THE VISUAL GUIDE TO
MINECRAFT

Dig into Minecraft with this (parent-approved) guide full of tips, hints, and projects!

JAMES H. CLARK
CORI DUSMANN
JOHN MOLTZ

The Visual Guide to Minecraft
Dig into Minecraft with this (parent-approved) guide full of tips, hints, and projects!

James H. Clark, Cori Dusmann, and John Moltz

Peachpit Press
Find us on the web at: www.peachpit.com

To report errors, please send a note to errata@peachpit.com
Peachpit Press is a division of Pearson Education

Editors: Clifford Colby and Robyn Thomas
Production Editor: Dennis Fitzgerald
Compositor: Maureen Forys
Indexer: Valerie Haynes Perry
Copyeditor: Scout Festa
Proofreader: Patricia Pane
Cover design: Mimi Heft
Interior design: Maureen Forys and Mimi Heft

ISBN 13: 978-0-134-03315-0
ISBN 10:   0-134-03315-9

9 8 7 6 5 4 3 2 1

Printed and bound in the United States of America

Dedication

To my pterodactyl and smilodon. Sometimes clichés are
suitable: The world is yours.   —*James H. Clark*

To all the kids and teens who share their wonder with
me—I truly couldn't do this without you.   —*Cori Dusmann*

To my son, Hank, who got me into this amazing game.   —*John Moltz*

Acknowledgments

Jennifer—my wife, my partner. To say her expertise, excitement, love, and support is nothing short of amazing would be an understatement.

Yes, their names appear on the cover, but it bears repeating: This book wouldn't be what it is without John and Cori. Cori's kindness, wit, wisdom, and encouragement in game and out have made this journey enjoyable. I'm honored to call her a friend.

Robyn, Cliff, and Scout—for their guidance throughout. And just as important as the words are the look and presentation: Thanks to the design and production crew.

—James H. Clark

Thanks to Xander (Lex/wrednax), who has been a silent partner but deserves full billing, not just for redstone expertise and contributions, but for putting up with the insanity that descends when a book is being born. A mom truly couldn't be luckier than I am.

John and James, with their unique voices and experiences, make this book all the better. Thanks to Cliff, Robyn, and all the team for pulling all the strings together.

James, with the insight and wisdom that comes from close friendship, knows when to listen, cheer, joke, or simply set me back on my path—there were many times I would have faltered without his support.

Rawcritics is my amazing Minecraft community, filled with fantastic friends who have contributed in innumerable ways, from edits and project help to being on the receiving end of my crazy more than once. You guys are amazing and always there for me, and I can't thank you enough.

Finally, to my mom, my family, my friends—there's no way I could do this without each and every one of you; thank you.

—Cori Dusmann

My thanks and love to my wife for encouraging me to quit working for The Man so I could pursue a career in writing and ultimate fighting (I'll get to the second one someday). But mostly my work on this book is thanks to my son, Hank, without whom I never would have played Minecraft in the first place. Love ya, bud!

No thanks to our dog, Grant. He just eats things he shouldn't and barfs them up at 5 a.m. BAD DOG! No, that's mean. Here. Have a biscuit.

Thanks to Cliff, Robyn, James, and Cori for putting up with me, the noob.

—*John Moltz*

Contents

PART 1: INTRODUCTION

Chapter 1: Getting to Know Minecraft. 3

Chapter 2: Surviving Your First Day. 15

Welcome to the World of Minecraft

Calling all miners, builders, explorers, designers, engineers, crafters, farmers, creators, and anyone with a sense of adventure—untold wonders await!

For over five years, Minecraft has been a source of wonder and adventure for players of all ages. Constantly evolving, with new creatures, blocks, and ways to play, this game that has no rules and no goals has captured the hearts and the imaginations of millions of players around the world.

Whether you have been mining and crafting for years or are just learning what a creeper is, there is always something new to discover and learn. With regular updates that add fresh features and all sorts of mods, Minecraft is a game that is always changing.

One thing that stands out about Minecraft, compared to other games, is that there are no rules, no goals, no storyline that you need to follow. You get to decide how you're going play, set your own goals, and play by your rules. Interested in designing and settling down in your own castle, village, or farm? You can build anything your imagination can conjure. Want to go exploring and find temples, fortresses, and caverns filled with treasure and monsters? Gear up and head out on a quest. Interested in creating automated machines to do some of your work for you? Explore the world of redstone, Minecraft's equivalent to electricity and circuitry. The options and opportunities are endless.

Mining, Crafting, Creating, and Exploring

This book is an exploration of a variety of aspects of Minecraft, from the basics and how to get started to an encyclopedia of items and mobs. In these pages, you'll find detailed instructions on how to survive your first night, design and build an epic home, and the ins and outs of redstone.

You'll find projects, information, tips, and tricks organized into four sections: "Information," Encyclopedia," "Structures," and "Redstone." You can start at the beginning and work your way through, jump to the beginning of any section and start there, or pick and choose what you'd like to learn about.

Computer, Console, Tablet

When Minecraft was designed, it was a game to be played on a computer and ran on the Windows, Mac, and Linux operating systems. Now players can play on Xbox 360 consoles, as well as on tablets and smartphones.

This book focuses on the original Minecraft game as designed for computers. Although the other versions share many components of the full game, there are differences, and those versions are often more limited. At the same time, many of the strategies and basic gameplay are so similar that you'll be able to use what you learn here whether you're playing on Xbox, Xbox One, PlayStation 3 or 4, tablet, smartphone, or computer.

A Note to Parents

(...and grandparents, aunts and uncles, teachers, and all other Minecraftian grown-ups)

If you have a Minecrafter in your life, you are likely already familiar with the all-consuming passion they have for the game. You may be wondering what makes kids so drawn to it, and how to manage their obsession and help them have some balance in their life.

Minecraft by its very nature is an open-ended, creative game that is inviting and liberating. The reality is that many kids now have fewer opportunities to just play freely. Days are long and often filled with extra classes and activities, and even free play can be more restricted than in past generations. Kids don't have the same freedom to go out into the world, explore, take chances, make mistakes—so games like Minecraft are more valuable than ever. This is not at all to say that games should replace outside time, extracurricular activities, family time, sports, crafts, or any of the other awesome ways kids pass time, play, and learn. It does, however, help to explain the allure of Minecraft.

Somewhere in all the rest, we have forgotten that for kids, play is work. It is the most important work of all. Through play, kids can learn much more in terms of larger life skills than they ever do in a classroom—about all sorts of things, social connections, how to get along, cause and effect. And when they use a creative, open game like Minecraft, they are suddenly back to doing what comes naturally: learning through play.

In Minecraft, kids can take those chances and risks and face the consequences. They create worlds that come completely from their imagination, and they, and they alone, are the master of their domain. This gives them pride in their work and a feeling of responsibility, things we want to see and nurture in our children.

On the flip side, because kids are so invested in their Minecraft world, and since they create things that carry personal weight and meaning, they can become fixated on it. This isn't necessarily a bad thing; they are showing responsibility to what is essentially their work. Parents see it as an addiction, particularly when Minecraft is all their children want to talk about, and it can be an issue. Balance is important, setting times to play and times to move on to other activities is vital.

Letting your child share their passion with you is a great way to connect. Have them show you their work, see what they are proud of, and prepare to be amazed at what they've been up to when you think they've been merely playing a game. There is much more to Minecraft than you would guess at first glance, which is why it has been appearing in classrooms around the world, why adults are as swept up in playing as kids, and why it has become a worldwide sensation. Check out Cori Dusmann's book The Minecraft Guide for Parents (Peachpit Press, 2014) for more down-to-earth advice for parents of children playing Minecraft.

Introducing Your Guides

All three of the authors are parents. We've been drawn into the thick of the game not just because we have kids who play (James has been playing since his daughter was born), but because we love and play Minecraft ourselves. We bring varied Minecraft backgrounds, from hosting a family server to being staff on a large public server. Between the three of us, we have vast knowledge and hands-on experience of Minecraft and of other games, gaming culture, online communities, computers, coding, education, and child development. Drawing on this pool of knowledge and expertise, we've collaborated to create a kid-friendly collection of tips, tricks, and strategies that will also help adults who are helping kids navigate this complex and creative game.

James H. Clark is the production coordinator at the Lakeville Journal Co., a group of independently owned community newspapers. In addition to his role at the Journal, he is an independent designer, working in both print and web media. In 2010, James encountered Minecraft in its alpha phase and joined a fledgling online community, where he quickly became an administrator. His sense of humor and his broad knowledge and approachability have earned him the ironic nickname "old man" within the community, and he has become mentor, teacher, and support for many of the players, young and old. James lives in Connecticut with his wife and daughter.

Cori Dusmann, author of *The Minecraft Guide for Parents,* is an educator, writer, and homeschooling gamer parent who lives in Victoria, B.C., with her awesome 15-year-old writer, gamer, and Tumblr addict. With a BA in Child and Youth Care (counseling), Cori has spent over 20 years working with children in a variety of settings. Working predominantly with children with challenging behaviors, Cori has found games to be a source of common ground, and no game more so than Minecraft. In addition to her child-wrangling skills, Cori is a writer and reviewer. She regularly writes reviews for *Quill & Quire,* the Canadian publishing industry's monthly magazine, and her reviews have been printed in the *Vancouver Sun,* the *Globe and Mail*, and the *National Post.*

John Moltz grew up before the personal computer revolution, so he played with computers made out of cardboard boxes to pass the time until they were commercially available. After working in corporate technology for over 15 years (three of which he actually enjoyed), he quit his job in 2012 to become a freelance writer because money can make you only so happy. Writing, on the other hand—that'll make you miserable forever. John's work has appeared in *Macworld* magazine, *The Magazine, TidBITS,* and other places where fine nerdery is appreciated. He lives in Tacoma, Washington, with his wife, son, and gigantic poodle.

How to Download the Book's Videos

Purchasing this book gives you access to more than 3 hours of downloadable videos created by the book's authors.

1. Go to www.peachpit.com/register and create or log in to your account.
2. Enter the book's ISBN (978-0-134-03315-0), and click Submit.
3. On the My Registered Products tab of your account, you should see this book listed.
4. Click the Access Bonus Content link to access your videos.

Once you download the videos, you can view them on a computer, tablet, or smartphone.

PART 1:

INTRODUCTION

Minecraft is as fun as it is initially hard to understand. In this day and age of app stores, a game that you buy from a website and that requires other software to run it seems almost arcane. And the buttons. Oh, so many buttons. What do they all do?

Getting the game installed is just the first hurdle. The game comes with no real instructions, so surviving your first day in Minecraft can be a walk in the dark. Hopefully not literally, because that's when the bad things come out.

Don't worry. In the sections that follow, we'll not only explain how to get and install the game and survive your first day, but also go through how to expand the game. You'll see how to install add-ons, install and play modified versions of the game, and set up your own server in no time—or about 40 pages, whichever comes first.

Getting to Know Minecraft

Minecraft has been described many ways, but I like to call it a first-person adventure and builder game. Created by Mojang in 2009, it combines the building capabilities of Lego with a first-person shooter interface and puts them in an open, varied, and vaguely mysterious setting. Using a multitude of different materials (represented as blocks), players build tools and structures that help them survive and thrive in a seemingly endless world populated by animals, nighttime terrors, and a handful of scattered villagers.

And thrive you can. It's a cliché, but the cliché is true: The only limit in Minecraft is the player's imagination—and possibly parental screentime limits. Dedicated players make not only a variety of devices and buildings but entire cities and worlds. Third-party developers have expanded the options by making their own modifications to the core game, allowing for new building blocks, new recipes for crafting, and new environments and non-player characters (NPCs). It's almost infinitely extendible if you have the skills.

In the game, you harvest blocks by digging, chopping, or mining with various tools. Once harvested, the blocks have any number of uses. Items can be combined to make other things: weapons, devices, buildings, elevators, computers, and apparatuses for mining, farming, and collecting experience points that can then be used to craft even cooler stuff...it just goes on.

Probably best to get started.

Getting the Game

Minecraft has been developed for three platforms: PC, mobile operating systems (iOS and Android), and Xbox. While they're all fun to play and more alike than they are different, this book focuses only on the PC version.

The PC version of Minecraft consists of two things: the application itself and a user account. The user account costs $26.95 (U.S. dollars) per user and can be purchased on Minecraft.net.

Downloading the Minecraft Launcher

Getting the Minecraft software is very easy. But you'll need some way of paying for it, so if you want to ask someone older to help you, it couldn't hurt. The important thing is getting the game and getting playing. Be goal-oriented!

1. Go to minecraft.net (**Figure 1.1**).

FIGURE 1.1 Minecraft.net.

2. Click the Get Minecraft button. You'll be prompted for some information.

3. Enter an email address and password (**Figure 1.2**).

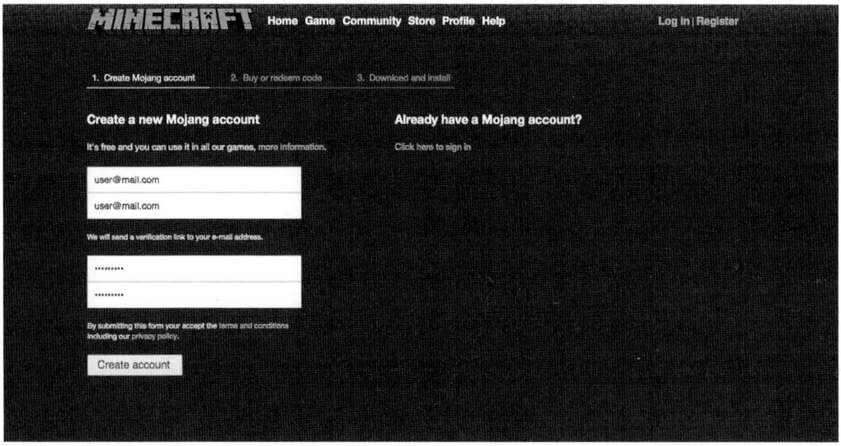

FIGURE 1.2 Enter an email address and create a password.

Mojang will send you an email to verify your email address.

4. Click the link in the email to continue the process.

5. Choose a Minecraft name and enter it (**Figure 1.3**). Fair warning: All the good ones were taken years ago.

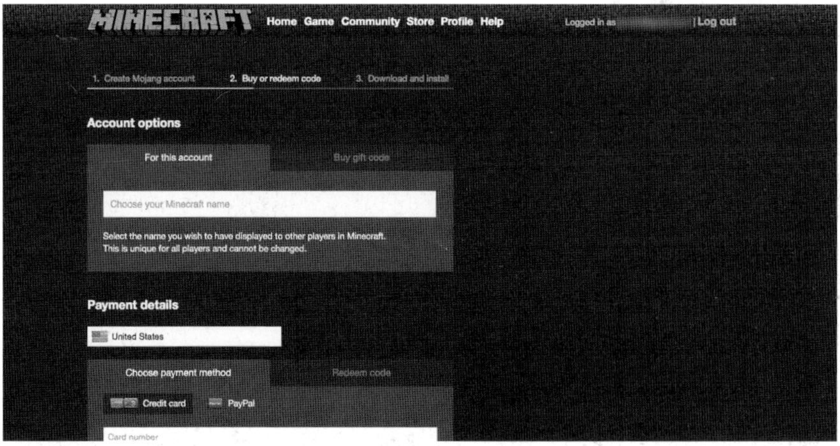

FIGURE 1.3 Name, rank, and credit card number.

If you intend to just play by yourself, your username will just be what you use to log in to the game. If you intend to play with others, however, it will be how they identify you in the game. Multiplayer is one of the great appeals of the game, so consider it likely that at some point you'll be telling others what your username is. Maybe "MAJORBUTTZ" isn't how you want to be known. Or maybe it's *exactly* what you want.

Two people can use the same username to play single-player games, but they can't play the same multiplayer game together.

6. Enter your payment details.

Your payment options include using a credit card or PayPal or clicking the Redeem Code tab to enter a redemption code from a prepaid Minecraft card.

Prepaid cards are available for purchase from some retailers. They make a great stocking stuffer if you can find a kid who isn't already playing Minecraft. I mean literally playing it right now.

After you provide payment information, you'll be directed to where you can download the Minecraft launcher. Minecraft.net will automatically direct you to the version for the operating system your computer is running.

> **NOTE:** You can download Minecraft again at any time if you get a new computer or want to play on multiple computers.

System Requirements

You can run Minecraft on a computer running Windows, OS X, or Linux. Base system requirements aren't heavy—2 GB of RAM, 200 MB of disk space, an integrated Intel HD or Radeon HD graphics card, and a processor capable of running up to 2.6 GHz. But to really enjoy the game, you'll want at least 4 GB of RAM, a recent graphics card, and a decent processor. Minecraft has a plethora of customizable video options that you can turn down, but don't shortchange yourself.

Minecraft for the PC is built in Java, so you'll need to be running a Java virtual machine to run Minecraft. (*virtual machine* is a fancy way of saying software that lets you run software not native to the operating system. Think of it like visiting a foreign country and having a translator.) Both Apple and Microsoft have discontinued shipping their operating systems with a Java virtual machine installed. If your computer doesn't have a Java virtual machine, you can download one from Java.com for free.

Word of warning: Although Mojang recommends Java 7 for running Minecraft, you may find that some modifications, known as *mods,* have been coded for Java 6 and will experience issues. Such is the perennial balancing act between updates for security and performance versus maintaining versions for backward compatibility.

Installing Minecraft

Depending on the type of computer you are running—Windows, OS X, or Linux—the installation process is slightly different.

1. Select your operating sytem from the following list and follow the directions.

   - On Windows, the file you download will be the launcher executable. Just save the file and then double-click it to run. Easy-peasy, the kitchen is sorry to report we're all out of mac-n-cheesey.

     Minecraft will create a folder for the application files it needs in order to run. On Windows, the location is %appdata%\.minecraft\.

   - On OS X, the Minecraft launcher application downloads as a disk image. Open the image, and then drag the launcher icon to the Applications folder to install Minecraft. Double-click the launcher icon to launch.

     Minecraft will create a folder for the application files it needs in order to run. On OS X, it will be in your user directory under /.Library/ Application Support/minecraft.

     If you ever need to find it in OS X, you'll need to unhide the Library directory. To do this, go to the View menu in the Finder and select View Options. Then select the Show Library Folder option.

   - On Linux, the download is a Java archive (.jar). As on Windows, just download the file and double-click it.

Minecraft will create a folder for the application files it needs in order to run. On Linux, the Minecraft directory will be in the root of your user directory.

When you run the launcher, you'll see some confusing command-line notifications about things it's doing to initialize itself. Don't panic. It's not required reading. There won't be a test on it. In fact, it's better if you avert your eyes. Sometimes it's better not to know how the sausage is made.

2. Once the launcher loads, enter your username and password (**Figure 1.4**).

FIGURE 1.4 Log in.

3. Click Log In.

Welcome to the launcher (**Figure 1.5**).

The launcher is an application that manages different Minecraft profiles for you and will download new versions of the game as they're released, depending on how you use it. As of this writing, Minecraft is at version 1.8. By default, the launcher will create a profile for you that's set to automatically use the latest release version of the game. Just leave it like that for now.

4. Click Play and the launcher will download the game for you. It could take a few minutes, depending on your Internet connection.

FIGURE 1.5 The launcher.

Using the Interface

Hey, you're in the game! You're not playing it yet, but you're getting closer to actually having fun (**Figure 1.6**).

FIGURE 1.6 Game Type menu.

The Game Type menu gives you the following selections:

- **Singleplayer:** Play an individual game.
- **Multiplayer:** Play a networked game.
- **Minecraft Realms:** Realms is Mojang's subscription service. It allows you to create your own Minecraft world that's hosted on their servers. With a Realms subscription, you can invite other players anywhere on the Internet to play in your world.
- **Options:** Allows you to change video, audio, multiplayer, and a host of other settings.
- **Quit Game:** Quit and exit out of Minecraft.

The small square icon with the globe allows you to change the language settings. The languages are almost innumerable. If you speak the language of the high elves of Middle Earth, you're in luck. Seriously, it's in there.

The application screen also features a different inspirational message each time you open it, from "Kiss the sky!" to "Free dental!" Other than that, the game does not come with any instructions, which is one of its signature charms and frustrations. Start playing and you're likely to have little idea what to do. We'll get to that, but first let's get comfortable with the controls.

Creating a New World

You don't have an existing world yet, so you'll be creating one. It is really easy.

1. Start a game by clicking Singleplayer (we'll get to the other two options later). You will be prompted to create a new world (**Figure 1.7**).

2. In the World Name field, enter a name for your world.

   You can use numbers to name your world, use names from your favorite fantasy books, whatever. Just know that you might create hundreds of worlds and if you use the default name, New World, over and over, it's going to get a little confusing.

FIGURE 1.7 A whole new world.

Choosing Options for Your World

Minecraft allows you to select the mode in which you want to play. There are four game modes:

- Survival, which is the default, means you'll have to search for resources on your own and fight bad creatures that hate you for some reason. The reason is never made clear. I like to imagine it's religious intolerance.

- Hardcore is like Survival but, well, harder, and you get only one life. This is probably the least used setting because who needs that pressure?

- Creative gives you access to infinite resources, makes you invulnerable, allows you to fly and destroy blocks with one hit, and lets you run commands that can do a lot of other things. This mode is great for when you're building that to-scale Western frontier town or Santa's village or the entire lost continent of Atlantis.

- Spectator is a game mode that was added in version 1.8, but it can be activated only by using cheats during the game. This mode allows you to fly around the game observing, but you can't interact with anything.

Click the Game Mode button to cycle through the available modes.

Not enough options for you? Click the Create New World Options button (**Figure 1.8**).

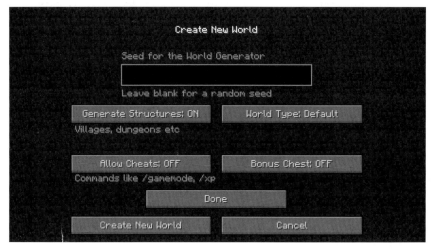

FIGURE 1.8 More world options.

You have lots of options to choose for your new world.

- Seed for the World Generator. At the top is a text box that allows you to put in a seed for the World Generator. A *seed* is a kind of loose blueprint for the world that says, for example, what kinds of biomes it will have in what sizes. You can find seeds online, but leave it blank for now.

- Generate Structures controls whether or not villages, temples, and dungeons are created (*dungeons* is something of a misnomer, because they're really mines).

- World Types lets you cycle through three options:

  - Default uses a varied set of biomes (forest, desert, mountainous, and more).

  - Superflat is a completely flat world with no varied biomes, trees, or ores (although it can be configured differently). Usually this is used in Creative mode to build structures or experiment rather than for normal gameplay.

  - Large biomes is just like Default but with larger biomes. Maybe you'll find that you like big biomes and you cannot lie. I'm not here to judge.

- Allow Cheats will let you use commands in Survival like you can in Creative.

- Bonus Chest gives you a head start by putting a chest with a few items in it near your spawn point. Your spawn point is where you start the game, either for the first time or where you restart it after you've been killed. Later you'll learn how you can move the spawn point. You might like to try a bonus chest for your first few outings, but purists eschew such indulgences.

Pick your poison and click Create New World.

Moving Around in Your World

Once in the game, you move around like in a first-person shooter. Using some simple keyboard keys will move you in any direction you want to go:

- W moves you forward.
- A moves you left.
- D moves you right.
- S moves you backward.
- Spacebar makes you jump.

You also have some action methods:

- Left-click to hit, chop, or dig something.
- Right-click to use something (control-click on a Mac).
- Double-tap and hold W to sprint until you run into something.

These key assignments can be changed at any time by pressing the Esc key, clicking Options, and then clicking Controls.

Paying Attention to Your Status Bars

Along the bottom of the game window, you'll see a row of hearts and a row of chicken legs (**Figure 1.9**). These indicate your health and food statuses, respectively (there is no thirst). Your health will drop if you get hurt, naturally, and your food status will drop slowly as you move around. Your food status will drop twice as fast if you're running. If your food status drops to zero, you'll start losing health, but you can't starve to death in normal Survival mode. You'll just be really easy to kill.

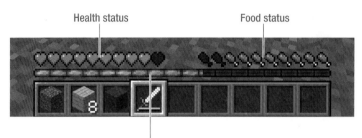

Health status   Food status

Experience points

FIGURE 1.9 Status bars.

Of course you can die in Minecraft. Oh, the ways you'll die! You can be killed by a monster, fall from a great height, drown, get blown up, go swimming in lava, and die in numerous other ways. Don't worry, you'll respawn.

Below the hearts and chicken legs is a line that shows your experience points. Experience points are gained by killing creatures or mining certain ores. They can be used later to enchant items to give them special abilities. But let's not get ahead of ourselves.

At the bottom you'll see a series of boxes. This is part of your inventory and will contain items you can use once you actually acquire them. In Figure 1.9, for example, the inventory contains a block of dirt, eight blocks of wood, a block of gray wool, and a sword.

Summary

If the interface seems intimidating right now, don't worry. It'll soon become second nature. The important things to remember are that the application you launch is the Minecraft Launcher, which manages the different versions of the game itself, and that games are either single-player or multiplayer. Beyond that, there are a variety of different settings, but you don't need to even touch them to enjoy playing the game.

Those are the basics, so let's not waste any more time. Let's play.

2 Surviving Your First Day

Welcome to the world.

It's morning and you are... somewhere (Figure 2.1). You could be on the side of a mountain, in a field, or in a forest. What's important is that time is of the essence. A day in Minecraft is 20 minutes long, so you have 10 minutes until night falls. What happens when night falls? That's when the bad things come out. No time to explain that, though. Let's go over what you'll want to accomplish before that happens.

FIGURE 2.1 A typical Minecraft setting.

Preparing for Night

Depending on where you start the game, your first day can be easy or it can be hard. The farther you have to go to find the things you need, the harder it's going to be.

At a minimum you'll need to:

- Collect some basic resources
- Assemble some tools
- Build your first home

Sounds easy, right? It usually is if you know what to look for and don't waste any time. Are you moving yet? You should probably get moving.

Collecting Resources

The first thing you want to do is find a tree. There are several kinds in Minecraft, but it doesn't really matter which one you use. Approach the tree and punch at the bottom block of the trunk by pointing the crosshairs (reticle) at it and pressing and holding the mouse button. Yes, you can harvest wood by punching a tree (**Figure 2.2**). Just like in real life. Er... well.

FIGURE 2.2 Punch that tree.

Using the same process, chop up all the trunk that you can reach, and you'll see the wood fall as little blocks. Walk over to the blocks to pick them up (gather at least four blocks of wood). Once you have the wood, you have to turn it into a useful form. To do that, press E to enter your inventory (**Figure 2.3**).

Your inventory is where the things you pick up or create are stored. Think of it like a backpack. Just one that can hold a lot of stuff.

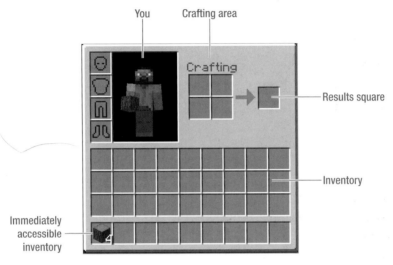

FIGURE 2.3 Your inventory.

Hey, that's you! That's what you—or as the character is known, "Steve"—look like in Minecraft. To the left of your image are four vertically arranged spaces where you can put items you wear, such as armor, which will help protect you against those bad things we talked about. You won't get to that on your first day, though. To the right of you is a 4x4 space for simple crafting. All the squares below your avatar are your inventory. You can hold up to 36 different kinds of items in various quantities. For most resources, you can hold up to 64 of them in each square. For tools, you can only hold one in each square. Any item placed in the bottom row can be used when you close the inventory by tapping the number of the space it occupies. Press 1 to use the item in the first square, 2 to use the item in the second square, and so on.

Assembling Tools

The pickaxe in Minecraft is the most basic tool. While an axe will cut wood faster and a shovel will dig dirt faster, the pickaxe will do both of those tasks. To make a wooden pickaxe you'll need three wooden planks and two sticks. Let's start by turning your raw wood into planks (**Figure 2.4**). Click the blocks of wood from your inventory to pick them up. Then click in any of the four squares in the crafting area to place them.

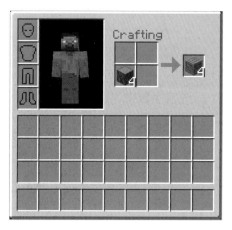

FIGURE 2.4 Making planks.

Minecraft helpfully shows you that you can turn those blocks of wood into planks in the results square on the right. You can still pull the blocks of wood out without creating the planks. But we need them, so click once on the planks to pick them up, and put them into your inventory by clicking any empty space there. To turn all the wood into planks, keep clicking on the results square until all your wood is used up, then put them in your inventory. Go ahead and do that. Raw wood might be good for ornamental use, but planks are more practical.

Planks can, for example, be turned into sticks. While wood blocks can be turned into planks by placing them in any square, most items in Minecraft require a *recipe*, an arrangement of certain items in a certain pattern, in order to create the resulting item. Place two planks in the crafting area, one above the other (if you're holding more than one of any item, you can place just one in a square by right-clicking instead of left-clicking). Those two planks will net you four sticks (**Figure 2.5**), so grab 'em and put them in your inventory.

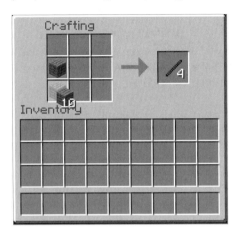

FIGURE 2.5 Making sticks.

The crafting recipe for a pickaxe is three planks across the top, with two sticks vertically underneath the middle plank. But, wait, that describes a 3x3 crafting area. Our personal crafting area is only 2x2. That's why you're going to need a crafting table (**Figure 2.6**).

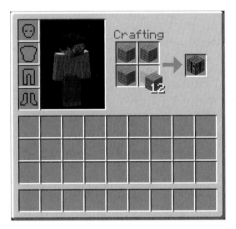

FIGURE 2.6 Crafting table.

Put one plank in each of the four squares of your personal crafting area, then grab the resulting crafting table by clicking it. In order to use it, you have to set it down somewhere, and in order to set it down somewhere, you have to have it in your row of immediately accessible inventory items. Click in one of the spaces in the bottom row to put the crafting table there. Now, with that position selected, point at a spot on the ground where you want to place the crafting table and right-click. Now point at the crafting table and right-click again. There's your 3x3 crafting area, so let's make that pickaxe (**Figure 2.7**). Remember, it is made by placing three planks across the top, with two sticks vertically underneath the middle plank.

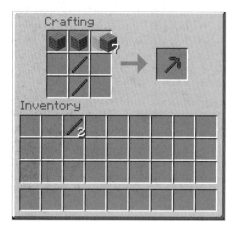

FIGURE 2.7 Making a pickaxe.

Now you can accomplish a lot more in the Minecraft world. Tools made solely of wood won't last as long as tools made of materials you'll find later, but they do get the job done.

Building a House

Your next order of business is to make yourself a place to hide when night falls. Later you'll find all kinds of fancy ways to make a house for yourself, but right now it's best to go with the original: a cave. Existing caves in your Minecraft world might already be populated with bad things, because caves are dark and bad things spawn wherever it's dark, so it's best to dig your own (**Figure 2.8**).

Find the closest hill or cliff face that's at least three blocks high, and using your new pickaxe, dig a two-block high entrance into the side. Keep digging into the hill until you have a decent roof over your head, maybe four or five blocks deep into the hillside (**Figure 2.9**). Notice that you'll pick up materials as you excavate, probably some dirt and cobblestone (the result of digging up stone). That's good, as you might need them for building materials later, and you'll definitely need some for a makeshift door.

FIGURE 2.8 This looks like a good spot to dig a cave.

FIGURE 2.9 Dig it.

It's also advisable to carve out at least one side of your cave home a little because some of those bad things can shoot at you, so you'll need to be able to stay out of their line of fire if they come looking for you (**Figure 2.10**). Once you've made a comfortable enough area—a floorspace about 4x4 will give you room to add some items later—you can make a makeshift door by placing a block of dirt or cobblestone across the opening to block the doorway when night falls. Leave only a 1x1 opening; bad things can't get through a 1x1 opening. Don't close the opening up all the way or you'll be left in the dark and you won't be able to see when the sun comes up.

FIGURE 2.10 Cozy!

Notice that in your inventory are the blocks you cut up and walked over. You automatically pick up items you walk over. This can become a management issue later as you dig more and more for resources, but for now these blocks might be valuable in building other things. You can drop things you don't want by putting them in your immediately accessible inventory, activating them, and pressing Q on the keyboard.

It's quite possible that all this will have taken you 10 minutes, in which case night will be falling soon. The sun moves in Minecraft, so if you can see it, you can estimate what time it is. If it's almost sundown, you might as well hole up for the night.

Lurking in the Night

While you're waiting for the sun to come up again in 10 minutes, let's talk about what those things are that might kill you. You're not going to sleep tonight anyway.

- **Zombies.** It's not clear if they want to eat your brains, but these are still your basic "Grr! Arrg!" types and are out to kill you. They need to get close in order to do that, so stay far away or hit them with anything you've got if they get close, preferably a sword. Don't eat the rotten flesh they drop. Why should I have to tell you that? What's wrong with you?

- **Skeletons.** They are archers, so keep a healthy distance. If you have to kill one, approach it at an angle or by zig-zagging. When killed, they may drop bones, arrows, or even a bow (the shooting kind, not the package-wrapping kind). Those items will come in handy. Be sure to pick them up.

- **Creepers.** The signature bad critter of Minecraft, creepers will explode when they get close to you, damaging you and the blocks nearby. It's best to kill them from a distance with a bow, once you get one, but you can kill them with a sword if you're fast. Sometimes creepers drop gunpowder. Creepers spawn only at night, but unlike zombies and skeletons, they are not destroyed by sunlight. When you head out in the morning, keep an eye out.

- **Spiders.** They attack you only when it's dark out, but sometimes they have a venomous bite that can drain your health. Spiders may drop string, which can be used to make a bow or a fishing rod, or a spider eye, which can be used to make potions.

There are others monsters you'll meet up with eventually, but zombies, skeletons, creepers, and spiders are the ones you're likely to encounter on your first night. In general, it's best to avoid them at this point if you can.

What Next?

If you've made your cave and you find you still have some time before night-fall, here are some accomplishments you can try for extra credit. Don't venture too far afield, though. You'll want to get back to your house as fast as possible when the sun starts to set.

Find Coal

Coal has a number of uses, but the one most pertinent for you right now is to make torches. Torches, as you might know, make light, and light keeps the bad things from spawning near you. Light also just makes it easier to see, and you'll need that when you go spelunking. Coal in Minecraft looks like stone but with black specks in it (**Figure 2.11**). It's easiest to find in an exposed cliff wall or in a cave. If it's up high, you can carve or build yourself a staircase to get to it.

FIGURE 2.11 Coal.

To make torches, place one coal over one stick. Place torches on a block by holding the torch, pointing where you want it to go, and right-clicking.

Find Food

The easiest way to start out is to be on the Paleo diet: meat, and lots of it. You can kill animals with your fists, a piece of wood, a pickaxe, whatever, but it's a little easier to kill them with a sword. Now, look for a cow, a chicken, a sheep, a rabbit, or a pig and hack away at it until it gives up its life-sustaining flesh. These are the only animals that drop meat when you kill them (rabbits don't always drop meat). Beef, pork, mutton, and rabbit are safe to eat raw, but raw chicken has a one in three chance of poisoning you (exactly the same odds as eating in the cafeteria at school). You can cook any of these meats in a furnace, which will remove the chance of poison and also satisfy more hunger. As a bonus, sheep will drop wool, cows (**Figure 2.12**) may drop leather, and chickens may drop feathers, all of which have their uses.

FIGURE 2.12 Don't you judge me, cowie. If push came to shove, you'd eat me, too.

If you have moral compunctions about killing pixel-based life forms, you can start a farm without too much trouble. You'll need two things: a hoe and seeds. You can fashion a wooden hoe by putting a stick in each of the bottom two center squares of your crafting table and a plank in each of the upper-left two squares. To get seeds, look for grass stalks (**Figure 2.13**).

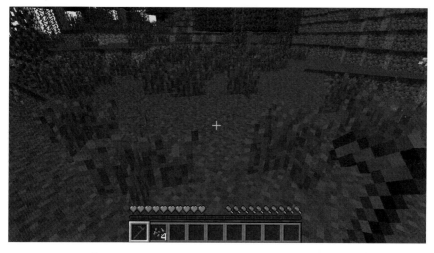

FIGURE 2.13 Grasses.

Each grass stalk you hack up has a chance to yield seeds. With your hoe, till a dirt square by pointing at it and right-clicking. Then plant the seed by holding it, pointing at the tilled square, and right-clicking. These will grow into wheat plants. When they turn brown, you can havest them by punching them and they'll drop wheat. Three wheat plants in a row in your crafting table will make a loaf of bread.

Some notes about farming: Animals will eat your wheat plants if you don't keep them away. If you put water close to your crops, they'll grow faster. You can make bonemeal from skeleton bones; place bonemeal on your crops to make them grow faster.

Build a Door

Instead of using that block of dirt for a door, why not spruce the place up with an actual door? Put six wooden planks in a three-up, two-across configuration to make the door, then place it by pointing at the threshold of your cave and right-clicking.

Make a Sword

A pickaxe will get the job done, but a sword is better for killing things. You can craft a wooden sword by putting one stick in a bottom square, with two planks in each square above it for the blade. More durable swords can be made with blades of cobblestone, iron, or other materials you're likely to encounter later.

Make a Chest

Your inventory holds only so many items, so it's helpful to have a place to put your extra stuff or just a safe place to keep things you don't want to lose. To make a chest, place eight planks in the outside squares of a crafting table, leaving only the center square empty (**Figure 2.14**). Place it in your cave and right-click to open it.

FIGURE 2.14 A box of holdings.

Make a Bed

Sheep don't drop meat, but they do drop wool when killed (they'll give more wool if you shear them instead, but that requires iron, which you don't have yet). With wool and planks you can make a bed, which will make night pass almost instantaneously. Place three blocks of wool horizontally over three planks to get your bed. Then place it in your cave home (the block you select will be where the foot of the bed is placed). To sleep, point at the bed and right-click. You can sleep only once the sun has gone down. No napping in Minecraft! Beds also act as new spawn points once you sleep in one. So you can determine where you want to respawn, if you die, by making a bed and sleeping in it.

Gather More Resources

While you're wandering around, you might see rocks with colored flecks in them. Dig them up and you'll have different ores, which you can use to create a variety of resources once they're smelted in a furnace. A furnace is made by putting cobblestone in the outside squares of the crafting area (just like the chest). You power the furnace by putting coal in the bottom square. Then put the raw ore in the square above it (**Figure 2.15**).

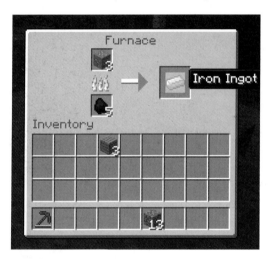

FIGURE 2.15 Smelting iron.

One of the more useful ores is iron, which can be crafted into more durable pickaxes, swords, and other implements, as well as armor to protect you in your upcoming epic battles.

The more you delve into caves or just dig into the ground, the more ores you'll find. Also, the more zombies, creepers, and skeletons you'll find. Make sure you have torches and a sword before you go very far underground, armor up at your first opportunity, and leave anything you don't mind losing in your chest at home.

It's easy to get lost in this game. One hill looks like another, one birch tree looks like another, and don't get me started on the cows. Making some kind of marker to help you find your home will be time well-spent. Climb the hill your cave is dug into, and, using any of the materials you dug up, make a stairway to heaven. You can use anything, but cobblestone stands out a little better because it's less likely to be naturally occurring (**Figure 2.16**). The more noticeable it is, the better.

FIGURE 2.16 Making your mark.

Accessing Your Achievements

While you were rushing around collecting items, making tools, and generally trying to save your bacon, you may have noticed that Minecraft applauded you a couple of times—when you first opened your inventory and when you first cut some wood. These are *achievements*. Although Minecraft doesn't have a help feature, achievements are meant as a means to guide you through play if you choose to use them.

To access achievements, press Esc on the keyboard while in the game (**Fig-ures 2.17** and **2.18**).

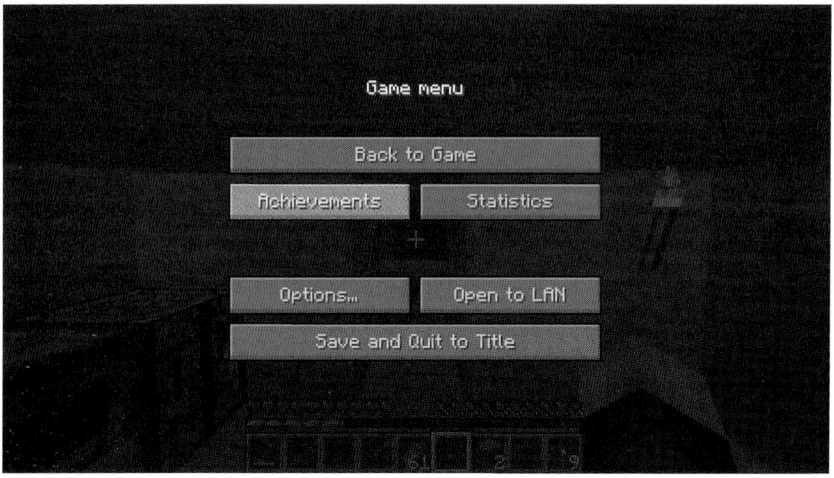

FIGURE 2.17 Achievements button on the Game Menu.

Then click Achievements (**Figure 2.18**).

FIGURE 2.18 So much to do, so little time.

Achievements might give you a hint about what to do next, but they don't really tell you how to do it. "Use planks and sticks to make a hoe" isn't a recipe. Fortunately, you can find recipes online at the Minecraft Wiki (http://minecraft.gamepedia.com/Minecraft_Wiki) or in other sources.

Summary

Surviving your first day in Minecraft means moving fast and getting down to business. Collecting wood and making yourself a place to hide are your top priorities. There will be plenty of time for calculated risks later in the game, but now's the time to play it safe: gather items, build protection.

So, did you make it? Did you survive your first day? Well, if you did, don't get cocky, kid. There are plenty of ways to die in Minecraft. You'll get yours eventually. When you do, all your possessions will fall where you die and you'll respawn with nothing. Your items will lie there for a while, but you'll need to race back to get them before they disappear. And whatever killed you will probably still be there...

But that's for another day.

Extending Minecraft

This is where things get crazy. The ways to extend Minecraft are almost as plentiful as the things you can do in the game.

As a parent, I can tell you that Minecraft playdates are definitely a thing. And according to the 10-year-old in my house, what's even more fun than playing with a friend is getting your dad to play, too, so you and your friend can gang up on him. Yes, I have been trolled by two laughing ten-year-olds.

Hosting a Game

There are several ways to host a game and play multiplayer Minecraft, ranging from easy to much less easy.

Setting Up a Local Network (LAN)

The easiest way to host a multiplayer game, and the one that requires the least investment in time and money, is simply opening the game you're playing to your local network (LAN). If your house has a Wi-Fi network, the game you host will be available for anyone on the network to join.

1. While in your game, press the Esc key to open the Game Menu screen (**Figure 3.1**).

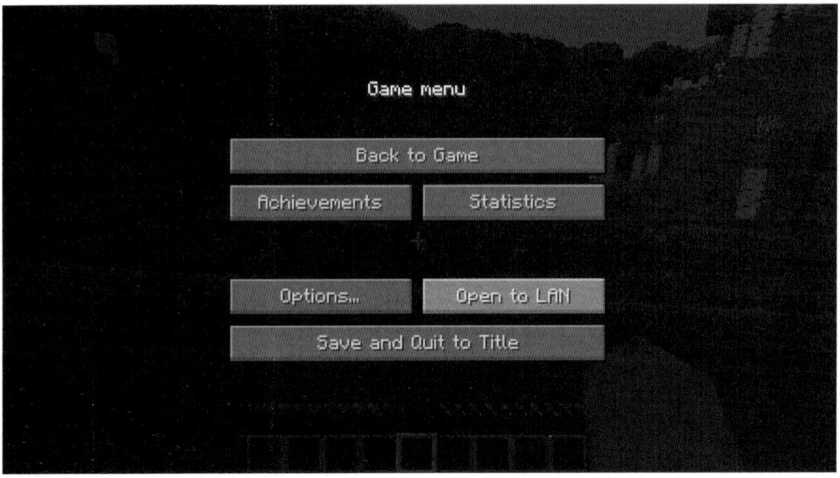

FIGURE 3.1 Open to LAN.

2. Click the Open to LAN button to display the LAN World options (**Figure 3.2**). You can choose two settings for the players that will join your game:

- The game mode: Survival, Creative, Spectator, or Adventure (a mode in which players cannot destroy most blocks)

- Whether to allow players to use cheats

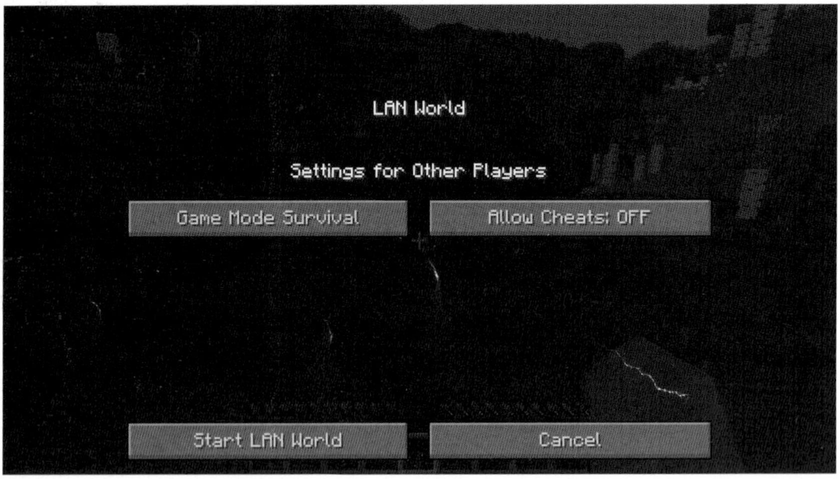

FIGURE 3.2 LAN play options.

3. Click the Game Mode button to cycle through the options, and select the mode you want for the hosted game.

4. Click Allow Cheats to toggle the setting on and off.

5. Click Start LAN World to save your settings and host the world.

Once you've opened your game on your LAN network, other players on your network can join.

6. The players joining the game select Multiplayer from the Game Type menu.

Minecraft scans your network for hosted games, and the game appears (**Figure 3.3**).

FIGURE 3.3 Logging in to a shared game.

7. The joining player clicks the hosted game and then clicks the Join Server button.

If the player joining receives an error, make sure you are both running the same version of Minecraft.

LAN sharing is easy and free, but the player hosting must be in and playing the game in order for it to work. What if I'm hosting, but I need to get back to, say, writing a book about Minecraft and my son still wants to play in that world? That's when you want a game that's hosted on a server.

Purchasing a Realms Subscription

For $13 US dollars a month, Mojang offers a subscription service, called Realms, on which you can create and host your own Minecraft worlds. You will need a Visa or MasterCard in order sign up for Realms, so if you need an adult, go grab one. After all, paying for things is what they're there for.

1. Go to www.mojang.net/realms to sign up for the service.

2. Click the Get Realms button to display a form to log in to your Mojang account (**Figure 3.4**).

   Note that a Mojang account is separate from a Minecraft account (although Minecraft is the most famous, Mojang has other games that it sells), so you will most likely need to set up a new one.

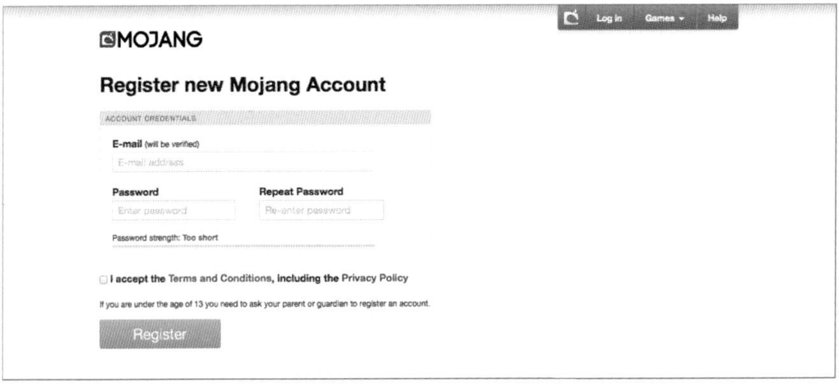

FIGURE 3.4 Creating a Mojang account.

3. Enter your email address and a password.

4. Re-enter your password to verify you entered it correctly, and click Register.

   Once you've created the account, you will need to associate your existing Minecraft account with your new Mojang account (**Figure 3.5**).

> **NOTE:** This will change your Minecraft login credentials to the email address and password you choose for your Mojang account. You will still retain your Minecraft user name, but it will no longer be what you provide to log in.

5. Enter your Minecraft login credentials, and click the button to associate the two accounts.

Mojang will then send an email to the address associated with your Minecraft account asking if it's OK to associate it with your new Mojang account.

6. Finish the process by clicking the link in the confirmation email that is sent to the address associated with your Minecraft account.

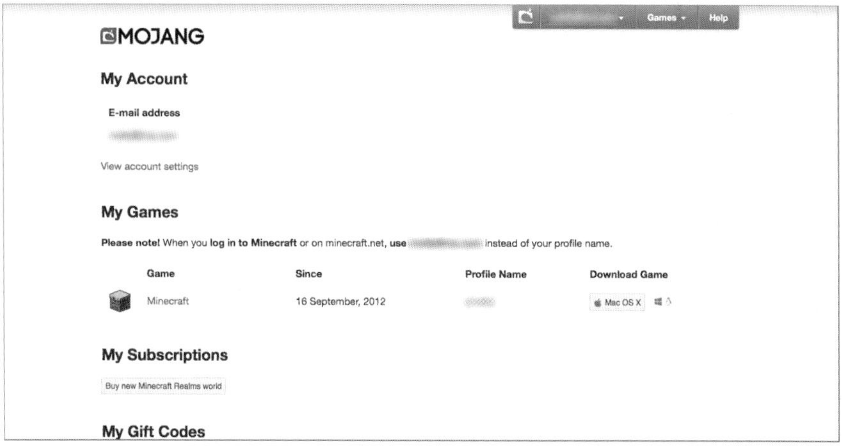

FIGURE 3.5 Your Minecraft and Mojang accounts are now merged.

7. In your account, scroll down to the Subscriptions section. Click the Buy New Minecraft Realms World button.

8. Choose your subscription plan and provide your payment information (**Figure 3.6**).

Only the host needs to have a subscription. The host can then invite other players to the realm.

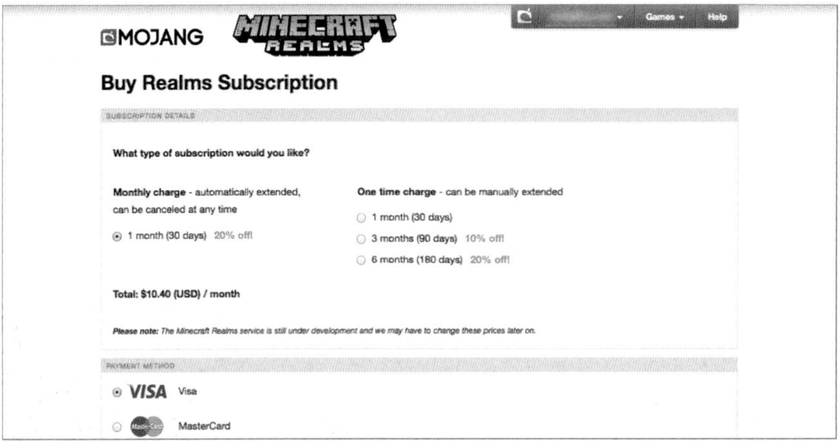

FIGURE 3.6 Subscription options, with sale prices.

Creating a Realm

Realms worlds have almost all the same features as regular Minecraft worlds. The host can use cheats but can't allow invited players to use them. Realms worlds also cannot be modded.

1. Return to the game application.
2. In the Game Type menu, click the Minecraft Realms button to display the Create Realm menu (**Figure 3.7**).

FIGURE 3.7 Create a realm.

3. Enter a name for your realm.

The Select Template (Optional) button allows you to select from a short list of world templates. You do not have to select a template.

4. Click Create (**Figure 3.8**).

5. Click the world you just created, then click Configure to display a menu (**Figure 3.9**) where you can add and delete players and edit the usual world settings.

FIGURE 3.8 Your new realm.

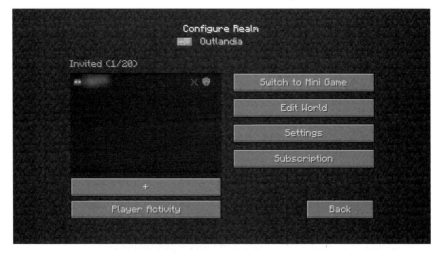

FIGURE 3.9 Minecraft is more fun with a friend.

Setting Up a Home Server

If you want more control over your Minecraft server, you can create one your-self for free.

Regardless of your operating system, you need to make sure that Java is installed on the computer that will be your server. The next steps differ for each type of operating system. The Windows setup is quite simple, but the OS X and Linus setups are more complex.

Windows

If your server computer is running Windows, go to http://Minecraft.net/download and click the link to download the server install under Multiplayer Server. Then just run the executable to get it running.

OS X

The process for setting up an OS X server is a little more involved.

1. Go to http://Minecraft.net/download and download the server .jar file.
2. Create a folder somewhere on your computer from which you want to run your server.
3. Open TextEdit and type the following into a new document. Make sure you type it exactly as shown.

   ```
   #!/bin/bash
   cd "$(dirname "$0")"
   exec java -Xms1G -Xmx1G -jar minecraft_server.jar nogui
   ```

   You might want to give your server more RAM. If you do, change the two instances of 1G in -Xms1G and -Xmx1G to another value, such as 2G.
4. On the last line, make sure that the file name minecraft_server.jar matches the name of the server .jar file you just downloaded. If it doesn't, change either the name of the file or the reference to it in the text file.
5. Change the document format to plain text by selecting Make Plain Text from the Format menu.
6. Save the document as **start.command** and place it in the same folder as the server .jar file.

7. Make sure you have execute permissions set on the start.command file by opening Terminal and then typing the following command:

```
chmod a+x
```

TIP: You can open Terminal by typing *terminal* into Spotlight.

8. Press the spacebar once to leave a space at the end of the command.
9. In the Finder, locate the start.command file and drag it into the Terminal window.

    This will insert the correct path and file name into the command you are going to run.
10. Press Return in Terminal.
11. Double-click the start.command file.

    The first time the server runs, it will create additional files in the folder. You might also see some error messages, which you can ignore.
12. Quit out of the server for now by pressing Command-Q.

Linux

If you are running Linux, the instructions are different depending on which distribution you are using. For more information, see http://minecraft. gamepedia.com/Setting_up_a_server.

Completing the Home Server Setup

From here, the configuration is the same for all platforms.

When running the server for the first time, you might see a message about not having agreed to the terms of the EULA (end-user licensing agreement).

1. Return to the folder you created. You'll see that one of the files Minecraft created is eula.txt.
2. Open the file in a text editor, and on the last line, change false to true (**Figure 3.10**) to indicate you agree to the terms, which you probably didn't read. I know I didn't.

```
#By changing the setting below to TRUE you are indicating your agreement to our EULA
(https://account.mojang.com/documents/minecraft_eula).
#Tue Aug 19 14:09:00 PDT 2014
eula=true
```

FIGURE 3.10 I agree to whatever.

At this time you can also change server settings in the server.properties file, which you will find in the folder you created. The default settings might be good enough to get started, but this is your server, after all. Make it yours.

To see a full list of the server settings, go to http://minecraft.gamepedia. com/Server.properties.

3. Once you're set, start up the server again by double-clicking the start. command file.

To play on the server, users on your network will need to know the IP address of the server machine.

4. Determine your IP address.

- On Windows, go to Run by pressing the ⊞-X. Type `ipconfig` in the command window and press Enter.

- On OS X, go into System Preferences, click Network, and select your active network connection.

- In Linux, run the terminal command `ifconfig`.

Joining the game is almost like joining a hosted game, except with more persistence.

5. Click Multiplayer in the Game Type menu.

6. Click Add Server.

7. Enter a name for the server and the IP address of the hosting machine **(Figure 3.11)**.

You can join from the same machine the server is running on (although you may find performance is slower). To do so, type in **localhost** for the Server Address.

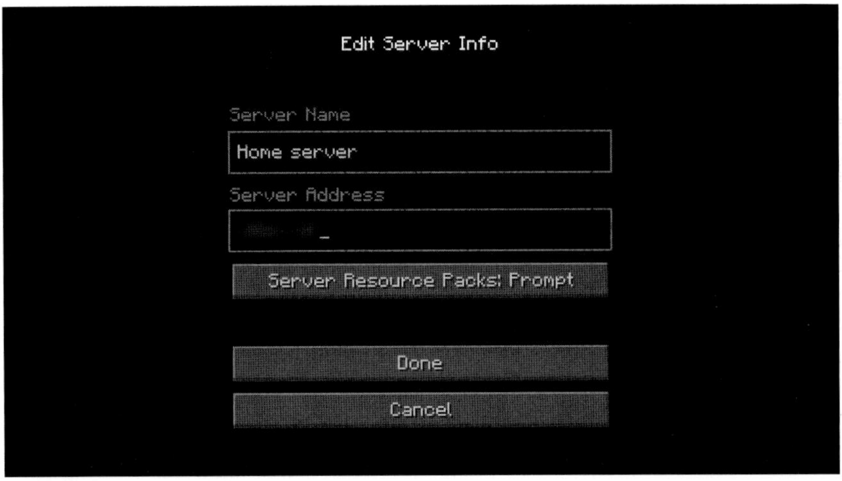

FIGURE 3.11 Setting up the server connection.

5. Click Done and Minecraft will scan for the server. If you see a set of green bars next to the server name, you're good to go (**Figure 3.12**).

FIGURE 3.12 Ready to connect to the server.

NOTE: If you want to make your home server accessible on the Internet, you'll need to open a port on your router. This process varies depending on which router you have. You can find more information at: http://minecraft .gamepedia.com/Tutorials/Setting_u

Modifying the Game

Ready to get crazy? Minecraft's extensible nature can be aggravating and rewarding. The game itself will let you change textures and your player skin, but if you're willing to get your virtual hands dirty, you can add maps, additional ores, and whole new worlds. Let's start simple and work our way up.

Skins

Don't like the default look of your character? Mojang has you covered. Your appearance in Minecraft can be changed via a skin. A *skin* is nothing more than a small image file that works like a piece of papercraft. The image file contains every visible surface of your Minecraft character's body, and each one is mapped accordingly.

Skins can be downloaded from sites like the Skindex (www.minecraftskins. com), or you can make one yourself with an image editor. Log in to your account on Minecraft.net, and click Profile. There you'll find a reference skin that you can alter to your heart's content. Follow the instructions to download and edit the skin.

Once you have your skin, upload it to your account by clicking Choose File (**Figure 3.13**).

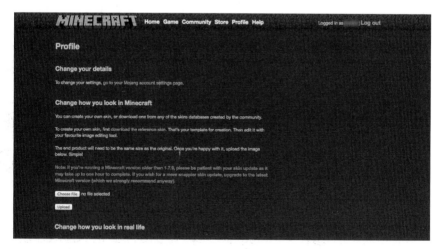

FIGURE 3.13 Change your skin on the Profile page.

Navigate to your file and select it. Then click the Upload button. Now your character will have a more personalized look on every Minecraft platform you log in to.

Resource Packs

You can change the look and sounds of the game by adding and managing resource packs.

Numerous resource packs are available to download on the Internet. The Minecraft forums are probably the safest place to do so. Minecraft's popularity has sparked nefarious websites that entice users to visit by claiming to be hosting Minecraft resources. You can find resource packs at www.minecraftforum.net/forums/mapping-and-modding/resource-packs.

One of the more popular ones is a pack that changes textures, called Faithful 32x32.

Once you've found a resource pack you're interested in, you need to get it on your computer.

1. Download the resource pack to your computer.

    You'll find that many independently developed Minecraft modifications are hosted on advertising-based file download services such as AdFly. When you click the link in the forum post, you may be redirected to a deliberately confusing page (**Figure 3.14**).

FIGURE 3.14 What do I click?

For AdFly, one of the more popular services, the download link will appear in the upper-right corner after 5 seconds. Click carefully.

Once you've downloaded the resource pack, you have to install it. Do not unzip it unless otherwise instructed, because Minecraft reads it in that format.

2. On the Game Type menu, click Options and then click Resource Packs.

This is your list of installed resource packs. There might be only one, the Minecraft default.

3. To add a new one, open the directory where resource packs are stored by clicking the Open Resource Pack Folder button. Drag the file you down-loaded into that folder.

4. Click Done.

5. Click the Open Resource Pack Folder button again to see the list of resource packs. There is your new resource pack (**Figure 3.15**).

FIGURE 3.15 Resource acquired.

Now you need to activate it.

6. Hover over it and click the right arrow that appears to move it from Avail-able Resource Packs to Selected Resource Packs.

You can install multiple resource packs at a time (the Default pack cannot be removed), but be warned: Some may not work and play well with oth-ers and may prevent the game from fully loading.

You can deactivate a resource pack that you no longer need or that is not playing well with others.

Hover over it in the Selected Resource Pack list and click the left arrow.

Faithful 32x32 will take the scene that appears in **Figure 3.16**...

FIGURE 3.16 Unaltered Minecraft.

...and make it look like **Figure 3.17**. This is just a subtle example of what skins can do.

FIGURE 3.17 The effects of Faithful.

Maps

Are you finding that the random maps of biomes that Minecraft generates are boring or frustrating? I hear you. Fortunately, there's a cure. You can download and install custom maps.

You can find many in the Minecraft forums at www.minecraftforum.net/forums/mapping-and-modding/maps.

Or you can find some in the Minecraft World Map site at www.minecraftworld-map.com.

Before you start downloading, it's time to get a little more familiar with what's in that Minecraft folder that gets created during installation (**Figure 3.18**).

Name		▲	Date Modified	Size	Kind
▶	assets		Aug 10, 2014, 9:27 AM	--	Folder
▶	config		Aug 21, 2014, 4:30 PM	--	Folder
	launcher_profiles.json		Today, 5:06 PM	787 bytes	Plain Text File
	launcher.jar		Today, 5:06 PM	4.8 MB	Java JAR file
	launcher.pack.lzma		Today, 5:06 PM	1.1 MB	LZMA File
▶	libraries		Aug 21, 2014, 3:23 PM	--	Folder
▶	logs		Today, 5:06 PM	--	Folder
	options.txt		Aug 21, 2014, 4:33 PM	2 KB	Plain Text
▶	resourcepacks		Aug 10, 2014, 9:26 AM	--	Folder
▼	saves		Today, 5:08 PM	--	Folder
▶	Creative		Today, 5:09 PM	--	Folder
▶	New World		Today, 5:08 PM	--	Folder
▼	versions		Today, 5:09 PM	--	Folder
▶	1.7.10		Today, 5:09 PM	--	Folder

FIGURE 3.18 The Minecraft folder.

You're already familiar with the resourcepacks folder. The saves folder is where Minecraft stores all your saved game data. Each game is saved in its own folder within saves. Conveniently, maps download as a complete folder. To install one, unzip it, if necessary, and drag the resulting folder into the saves folder. It will then appear in your list of saved games in the Singleplayer game list in the application.

Maps come in different types. Some are Survival maps just like the games you'd create within the application, but others are Adventure maps. Adventure maps are designed to play out a story, more like you'd play in a first-person shooter or other video game. Many blocks can't be broken, and you go through a series of challenges, from puzzle-solving to parkour, in order to complete the adventure.

E-land is a map that provides a city and several outlying areas for you to explore and make use of, such as two sports stadiums, an airport, and a shipyard (**Figure 3.19**). You can download it from www.minecraftworldmap.com/worlds/gp7tu#/939/64/-75/-4/0/0.

FIGURE 3.19 The E-land capital building.

Mods

Texture packs and maps are nice, but if you really want to turn the game up to 11, you want to run mods. Mods can add features to the game—new ores, new recipes, new creatures. They can be great and incredibly frustrating.

Why frustrating? Each mod has to be written for a specific version of the game. A mod written for Minecraft 1.6.4 might not work with Minecraft 1.7.10. The incredible popularity of YouTube mod reviews over the past few years means that you could easily take a shine to mod only to discover that it was written for an older version of Minecraft.

Fortunately, Mojang has made modding easier in recent releases by allowing you to more easily manage and run different releases of the game.

But the easiest way to play mods is to use Technic Launcher.

Technic Launcher

Technic Launcher is a Minecraft launcher built and maintained by a group of independent developers. The Technic platform allows people to bundle collections of mods with a particular version of Minecraft and download them as a package. The Launcher comes with several packs of mods pre-installed. Most offer enhanced crafting, such as the ability to make advanced machines like mining drills, jet packs, and lava-powered generators.

First you have to download the Launcher.

1. Go to www.technicpack.net.

2. Click the Download link, and select the download for your operating system.

3. Once it downloads, double-click the TechnicLauncher.jar file (**Figure 3.20**).

FIGURE 3.20 Log in to the Technic Launcher.

4. Log in with your Minecraft user ID and password, and the game home screen will load.

5. Use the arrows in the upper- and lower-left corners to scroll through the installed modpacks (**Figure 3.21**). The one in the middle of the column is the one selected to run when you click Play.

FIGURE 3.21 The Technic Launcher.

It's relatively easy to add more modpacks.

6. Click the Get More Modpacks button and the Technic website will load in your browser (**Figure 3.22**).

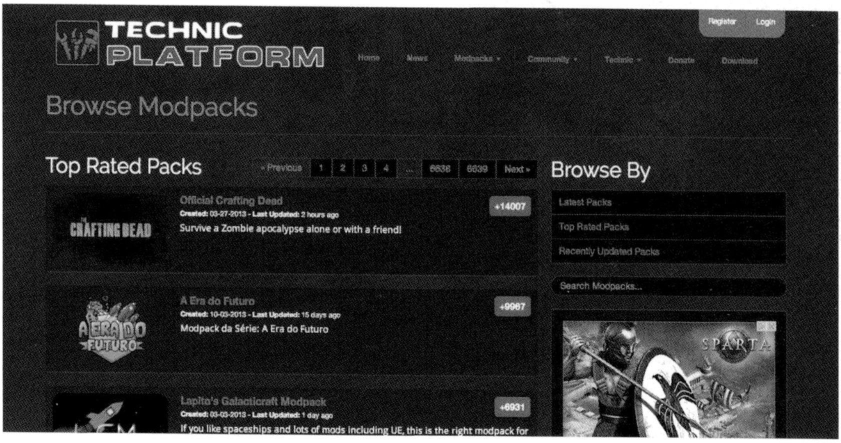

FIGURE 3.22 More modpacks than you can shake a stick at.

7. Hover over the Modpacks button and select Browse Modpacks.

8. Click the title of a modpack to open that modpacks page.

9. Copy the platform URL (**Figure 3.23**) and return to the Technic Launcher.

FIGURE 3.23 Pick a peck of modpacks.

10. Scroll through the list of modpacks until you get to Add New Pack.

11. Click the plus sign (+), and then paste in the platform URL.

The Launcher attempts to get the information for that pack.

12. Click Add Modpack.

> **NOTE:** To exit the Launcher, click the X in the upper-right corner.

Technic is the simplest way to play mods, but you have to choose someone else's pre-packaged collection. If you want to try your own combinations or run the hottest mod to hit downtown Minecraft, you'll need to run Forge.

Forge Mod Loader

Back in the dark ages, the world of Minecraft mods was like the Wild West. There were no standards, and mods were installed in a variety of arcane methods. Then along came Forge Mod Loader, a set of application programming interfaces that developers could use so that mods could be installed in a standard and relatively painless way. Mojang helped the process, too, by creating *profiles*. What are profiles?

1. Go back to the Minecraft Launcher.

2. Click the Profile Editor tab.

You'll see one profile there that's set to run the latest release of Minecraft (**Figure 3.24**).

FIGURE 3.24 Profiles.

But you can make more profiles, each running a different version of the game. Why is that important for mods? Remember that mods are written for specific versions. Consequently, so is Forge Mod Loader.

If you're getting a mod that's written for Minecraft 1.7.10, you need a profile for that version. First, set up a profile for that version in Minecraft.

3. Click New Profile, give it an appropriate name, and select 1.7.10 from the Use Version pop-up list (**Figure 3.25**).

4. Run it, and the Launcher downloads that version to your computer.

You don't actually have to play, just click Quit Game once the Game Type menu loads. Now you want to get the right version of Forge from the Forge downloads page (**Figure 3.26**).

5. Go to http://files.minecraftforge.net.

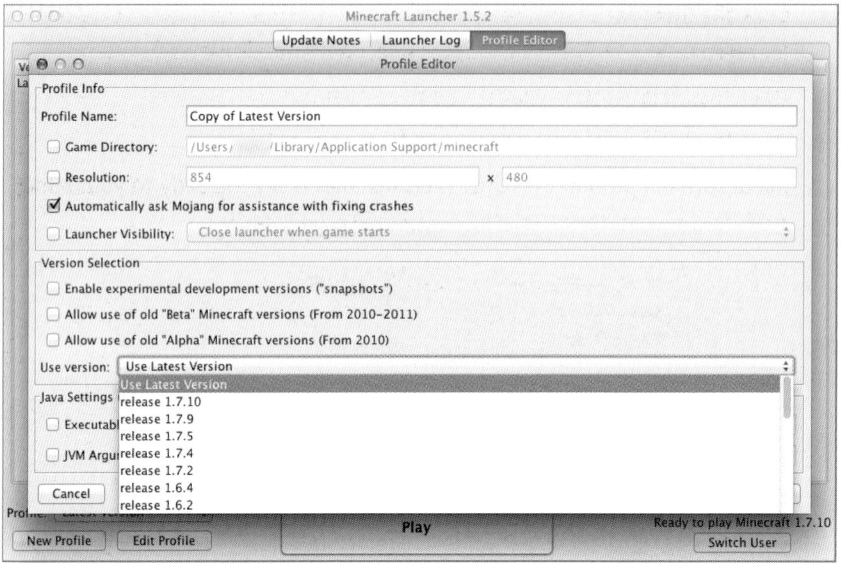

FIGURE 3.25 New profile.

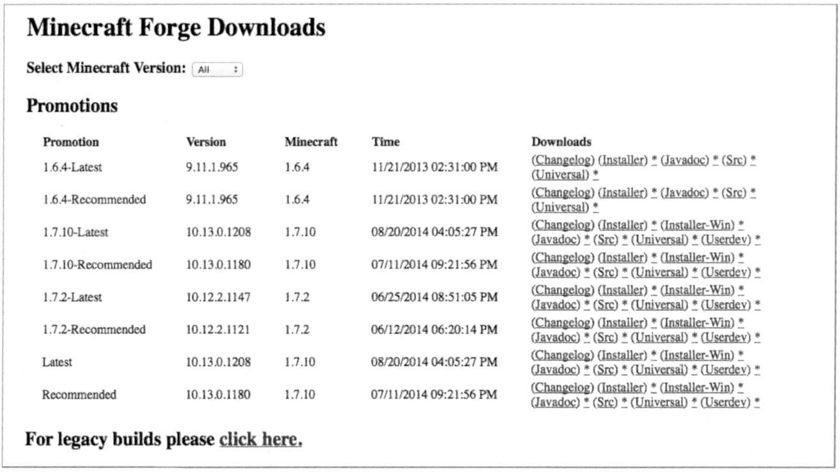

Minecraft Forge Downloads

Select Minecraft Version: All

Promotions

Promotion	Version	Minecraft	Time	Downloads
1.6.4-Latest	9.11.1.965	1.6.4	11/21/2013 02:31:00 PM	(Changelog) (Installer) * (Javadoc) * (Src) * (Universal) *
1.6.4-Recommended	9.11.1.965	1.6.4	11/21/2013 02:31:00 PM	(Changelog) (Installer) * (Javadoc) * (Src) * (Universal) *
1.7.10-Latest	10.13.0.1208	1.7.10	08/20/2014 04:05:27 PM	(Changelog) (Installer) * (Installer-Win) * (Javadoc) * (Src) * (Universal) * (Userdev) *
1.7.10-Recommended	10.13.0.1180	1.7.10	07/11/2014 09:21:56 PM	(Changelog) (Installer) * (Installer-Win) * (Javadoc) * (Src) * (Universal) * (Userdev) *
1.7.2-Latest	10.12.2.1147	1.7.2	06/25/2014 08:51:05 PM	(Changelog) (Installer) * (Installer-Win) * (Javadoc) * (Src) * (Universal) * (Userdev) *
1.7.2-Recommended	10.12.2.1121	1.7.2	06/12/2014 06:20:14 PM	(Changelog) (Installer) * (Installer-Win) * (Javadoc) * (Src) * (Universal) * (Userdev) *
Latest	10.13.0.1208	1.7.10	08/20/2014 04:05:27 PM	(Changelog) (Installer) * (Installer-Win) * (Javadoc) * (Src) * (Universal) * (Userdev) *
Recommended	10.13.0.1180	1.7.10	07/11/2014 09:21:56 PM	(Changelog) (Installer) * (Installer-Win) * (Javadoc) * (Src) * (Universal) * (Userdev) *

For legacy builds please click here.

FIGURE 3.26 Forge downloads.

6. Click the link for the installer for the version of Minecraft under the Downloads column (it's best to choose the recommended release).

Once the installer downloads, you need to run it.

7. Double-click the download to run it (**Figure 3.27**).

8. Make sure the path in the Forge mod installer is set correctly to your Minecraft folder, and then click OK to run the Forge installer.

FIGURE 3.27 Forge installer.

The installer runs. It copies the folder for the right version of Minecraft, renames it with "Forge" in the name, and installs its components in that folder.

So far all you have is a new version folder.

9. Run Minecraft again and select that profile. It will appear as "Forge" in your list of profiles.

10. Click Play.

Since this is the first time Forge is running, it does some setup; in particular, it creates a "mod" folder in your Minecraft folder. You'll know everything's good so far if there's a Mods button (**Figure 3.28**) on the Game Type menu.

FIGURE 3.28 Success!

11. Quit the game yet again, and now let's find a mod.

One of the best sources for mods is the MCF Modlist, at http://modlist.mcf.li.

The MCF Modlist helpfully keeps listings of mods by version.

12. Click the List menu at the top of the page, and you can see each version and the number of mods the site has listed for that version.

Let's try one out. How about BattleTowers (**Figure 3.29**)?

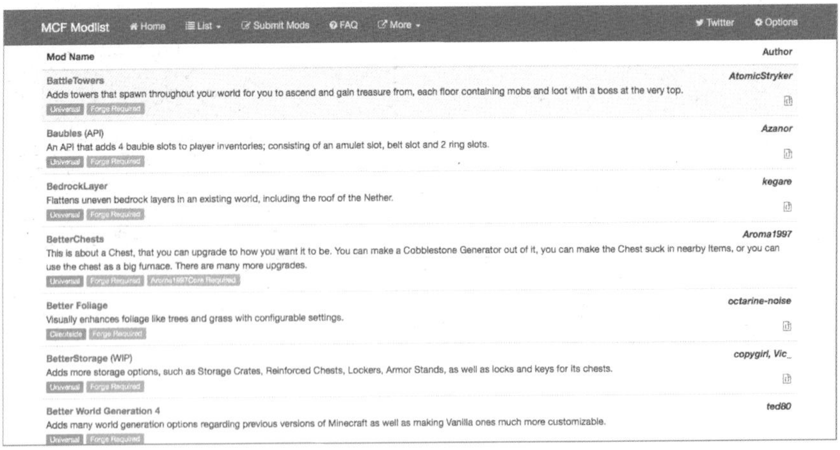

FIGURE 3.29 Battle Towers.

Ooh, that sounds good. They're *towers* that you have *battles* in! Hard to go wrong.

13. Click the title of the mod and it will take you to the developer's page for that mod.

Many of these are postings on the Minecraft forum and can be confusing. Usually the developer will keep the first page of the forum post up to date with the latest release information and download links for the mod. Again, most use an advertising-based hosting service for the files.

Once you've downloaded the mod, you need to find it in your file manager. Some mods have to be unzipped and some don't. Check the developer's installation instructions to see. If the developer doesn't provide good instructions, just try it both ways. It won't harm anything.

14. Drag the mod into the mods folder in your Minecraft folder. Hang in there, you're almost playing.

15. Open Minecraft again and play the Forge profile.

16. Click the Mods button and you can see if your mod is installed. If it is, you're ready to play (**Figure 3.30**).

17. Click Done.

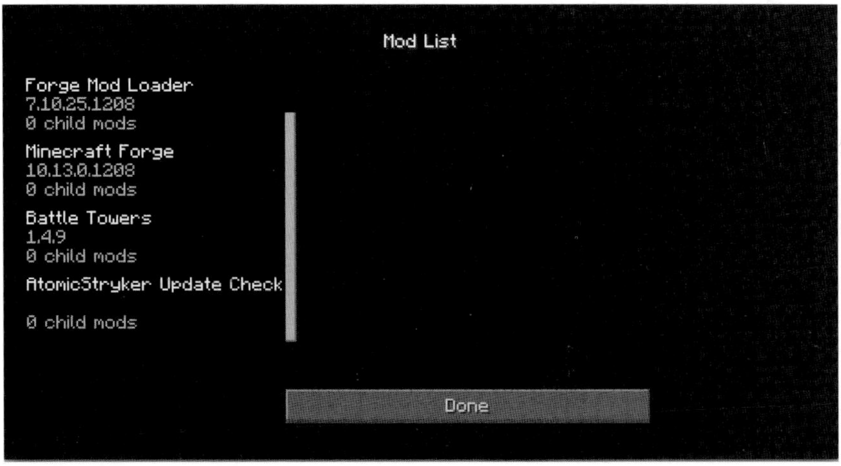

FIGURE 3.30 Ready to play!

You've taken your first step into a larger and more bewildering world. If you're looking for someone to separate the wheat from the chaff for you, a host of YouTube channels are dedicated to reviewing Minecraft mods: Try the Diamond Minecart (www.youtube.com/user/TheDiamondMinecart), SkyDoesMinecraft (www.youtube.com/user/SkyDoesMinecraft), and AshleyMarieeGaming (www.youtube.com/user/AshleyMarieeGaming).

Here are some recommended mods to help you get started:

- **The Lord of the Rings Mod:** http://lotrminecraftmod.wikia.com/wiki/ The_Lord_of_the_Rings_Minecraft_Mod_Wiki

   This mod adds orcs, elves, and all the other denizens of J.R.R. Tolkien's world to Minecraft, as well as mithril swords, Gondorian towers, and dwarvish caverns. The mod comes with a life-sized Middle Earth map featuring all the requisite biomes. Start in the Shire and see if you can make it all the way to Mordor. The mod is still in beta, but the plan is to turn it into an adventure map that lets players play out the events of *The Lord of the Rings*.

- **Too Much TNT:** www.minecraftforum.net/forums/mapping-and-modding/ minecraft-mods/1282366-1-6-4-too-much-tnt-mod-35-new-tnts

   Sometimes it's just fun to blow things up. This mod adds different and more powerful kinds of TNT to the game. Currently this mod is updated only for Minecraft 1.6.4. This is where the Profiles feature comes in handy; you can create a dedicated 1.6.4 profile.

- **Biomes O'Plenty:** www.minecraftforum.net/forums/mapping-and-modding/minecraft-mods/1286162-biomes-o-plenty-over-75-new-biomes-plants-and-more

   Minecraft comes with plenty of biomes, but Earth has more. With this mod you can get pretty much all of them, such as marshes, meadows, moors, and mountains. And that's just the *M*s.

Summary

There's really no wrong way to play Minecraft. Maybe you just like building in vanilla Minecraft, or maybe you want a tricked-out version with a dozen mods. The point is to make it what you want. The magic of the game is that you can.

PART 2

ENCYCLOPEDIA

Minecraft is an exciting, creative, and challenging game. More than many games, it allows players to play in exactly the ways that they would like to. Would you like to try to survive against the elements while battling monsters? Play a survival map and set it to be as challenging as you'd like. Are you more interested in building elaborate castles that tower high and are filled with marvelous automated creations? Log in to a creative map, and you'll have all the tools already in your inventory—and never worry about dying. Don't like playing alone? Fight other players, or team up with other builders on a server. You can set up your own server for you and your friends or find one online. The options and choices offered by Minecraft are almost unlimited.

Although it provides something for everyone, what Minecraft does not come with are directions, rules, or explanations telling players what the different items and blocks in the game are and what to do with them. There are countless tutorials online, and the Minecraft wiki (http://minecraft.gamepedia.com/Minecraft_Wiki) provides detailed information, but the amount of information can be overwhelming, and it can be difficult to know where to begin. More Minecraft information exists than can be contained in a single book, but here we're going to look at some of the basic facets of the game.

Minecraft Basics

As its name suggests, Minecraft is a game in which you need to mine for (and otherwise harvest or collect) materials, which you can then craft into other items and materials. These materials largely consist of blocks that can be placed and removed to create pretty much anything you can imagine. Blocks can be made of stone, wood, glass, clay, wool, or fancy ores, and many can be crafted into a variety of forms. Other items include tools, food, books, potions, and so much more. Add to this all the creatures in the game, both friendly and hostile, and there is a lot to learn and discover.

One of the amazing things about Minecraft is that it is constantly changing and being updated. The creators at Mojang regularly release updates that introduce new blocks, items, and mobs. Players can get a glimpse of what is coming with something Mojang calls *snapshots*. Snapshots are pre-release versions of an update that players can download and try out. Because of these updates, books like this sometimes don't have the most up-to-date information. Version 1.8 is being released as this book is being completed, so while we look at some of the newest additions, they may change a bit.

It's always a good idea to check the wiki for the most recent information on things you're interested in. Of course, there is also much that won't change—we take a look at some of those items, mobs, places, and more.

It's a Crafty Business

Although the name of the game is Minecraft, many more ways exist to gather materials than simply mining, but there's just one basic way to craft them. Using a crafting bench and recipes, plus the required materials, you can build almost any item found in the game.

Crafting Basics

Crafting is the act of taking materials (also known as *mats*) and, using the crafting grid in your personal inventory (accessed by pressing E) or a crafting bench, creating something new from those mats. For instance, a player could take eggs, sugar, wheat, and milk, and by placing them in specific places on the grid in their crafting bench, make a cake (**Figure 4.1**). The items needed to craft something and their specific placement are called a *recipe*. A recipe could be for making a food item, such as cake, or a piece of armor, such as an iron chest plate.

FIGURE 4.1 The recipe for a cake, in place on a crafting bench grid.

Crafting a bench is simple. It is likely the first thing you'll make, because you'll need a crafting bench to create almost everything else. You need four planks, which you get by punching a tree; the tree will drop logs. When you open your inventory (by pressing E), you will see a 2x2 crafting grid on the right. When you place your log in the grid in the left, it will show you planks with the numeral 4 in the box on the right, indicating that one log makes four planks. Pick up those planks by hovering your cursor over them and then clicking. Drag them to the grid again, placing a plank in each of the four grid squares. A crafting bench will show in the square on the right (**Figure 4.2**).

FIGURE 4.2 The crafting grid in your inventory, showing how to make a crafting bench or table using four planks.

To use a crafting bench, you need to place it by holding it in your hand and right-clicking. Right-click it again, and your 3x3 crafting grid will open. Place the recipe items in the correct squares on the grid, and then pick up the item that appears in the single box by clicking.

You can distribute items along the crafting grid by right-clicking and holding the button down as you move over the grid—this will divide the items evenly between the squares you move over. You can also use your right mouse button to divide a pile of the same item in half. If you want to make more than one of an item, simply place that many of each of the items in the recipe grid and pick up all of them at once.

Most recipes require that you put the items needed into specific spots on the grid, such as making a torch by placing a piece of coal or charcoal directly above a wooden stick. These are known as shaped recipes. Some others, like making dye from flowers, are shapeless—it doesn't matter where on the grid you put your items.

Basic Recipes

Many recipes for shaped objects are the same no matter what materials you use. If you're building stairs, you'll place six blocks in the crafting table in a step shape (**Figure 4.3**), although those blocks might be cobblestone, stone brick, sandstone, red sandstone, any of the six types of wooden planks, nether brick, or quartz. When we're looking at recipes that can be crafted with many materials, I'll just show one material and list the others that also could be used.

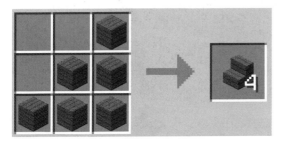

FIGURE 4.3 Stairs recipe: six blocks will give four sets of stairs. Stairs can be made from any of the six types of wood, cobblestone, stone brick, sandstone, red sandstone, nether brick, or quartz.

Types of Basic Block

Minecraft has close to 400 unique items. We can't explore them all here, but we can take a quick look at some of the basic ones.

Wood

One of the main blocks in the game, and one that is vitally important in order to progress, is wood. When you start, you're able to punch trees with your bare hands to collect wood logs. You'll use wood to craft your first tools, a chest and crafting bench, handles for torches, and doors for your house.

You can punch a tree to break it into logs, but once you make a crafting bench, you can craft an axe, which will make the job of chopping trees for wood much easier.

Wood logs can be crafted into planks, which can then be used to make stairs, slabs, fences, and doors. Each wood has its own color and appearance (**Figure4.4**), which is reflected in the planks and the items you craft.

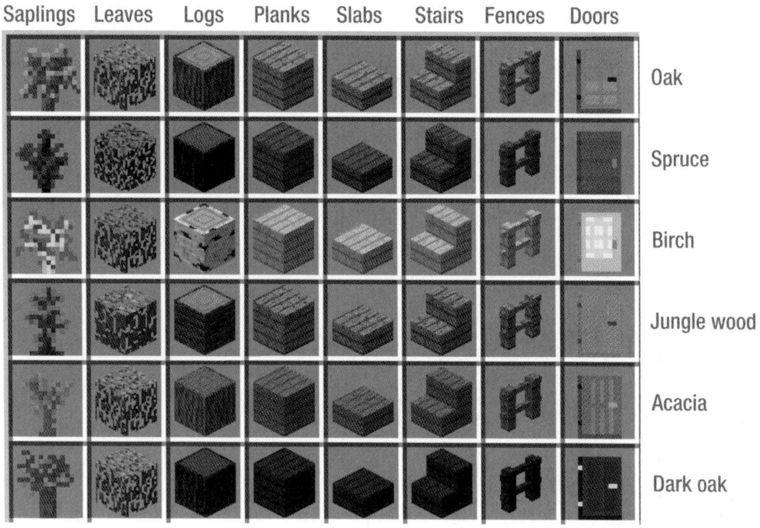

Saplings	Leaves	Logs	Planks	Slabs	Stairs	Fences	Doors	
								Oak
								Spruce
								Birch
								Jungle wood
								Acacia
								Dark oak

FIGURE 4.4 Types of wood, and how each appears in different forms.

When you cut down a tree, you need only cut the trunk; the leaves will slowly despawn, likely dropping a sapling or two as they do, which you can plant for new trees. Sprinkling bonemeal on planted saplings will help them grow faster. Dark oak trees will grow only if you plant four saplings in a 2x2 square. Spruce and jungle saplings can also be planted in this way for super tall trees.

Stone, Sand, Dirt, and Gravel

You can fairly easily collect dirt, gravel, stone, and sand (**Figure 4.5**).

Dirt and gravel can't be crafted into other forms, although dirt is needed for farming and is quick to dig with a shovel, making it useful for scaffolding. Coarse dirt, recently introduced, is a darker color and is found in the savannah, taiga, and mesa biomes. It can also be crafted with two blocks of gravel and two blocks of dirt, and when it is tilled with a hoe it becomes regular dirt.

Grass blocks, podzol, and mycelium are similar to dirt but with special properties. They all turn into regular dirt when they are dug up, unless you use a shovel that has been enchanted with Silk Touch, a somewhat rare enchant that allows you to harvest materials in their original form.

Row 1: dirt, coarse dirt, grass, podzol, mycelium, gravel

Row 2: cobblestone, smooth stone, stone brick, cracked stone brick, chiseled stone, mossy cobblestone, mossy stone brick

Row 3: granite, polished granite, diorite, polished diroite, andesite, polished andesite

Row 4: sand, sandstone, chiseled sandstone, smooth sandstone, red sand, red sandstone, chiseled red sandstone, smooth red sandstone

FIGURE 4.5 The dirt, gravel, stone, and sand blocks to be found and crafted.

Grass blocks are dirt with grass on the top. When placed, the grass will spread to other dirt blocks (although it won't spread to coarse dirt). Podzol looks more like composted dirt; it is a specialized dirt that can grow mushrooms. You can find mycelium only in the Mooshroom Island biome; it is also used to grow mushrooms. Like grass, and unlike podzol, it will expand to connected dirt blocks.

Gravel and sand (regular and red sand) share the unique property of being affected by gravity, meaning that when they are placed, they will fall until they reach a solid block; other blocks remain suspended where placed. You can smelt sand and red sand in a furnace to create glass (more on glass later) and use it to craft sandstone, smooth sandstone, and chiseled sandstone.

You can craft stone into many forms, which gives it great flexibility as a building material. When you mine stone, it will turn to cobblestone, unless you use a pick that has a Silk Touch enchantment on it that will leave it in its original form. You can return cobblestone to its smooth stone form by smelting it in a furnace, and it can be crafted into slabs, fences, and stairs that have a cobblestone texture.

Smooth stone can be crafted into slabs, and it can also be crafted into stone brick, which in turn can be crafted into stairs and slabs.

As of the version 1.8 update, stone brick can also be combined with vines to make mossy stone brick (previously only found in dungeons). Stone brick slabs can be crafted into chiseled stone, which had only been found in jungle fortresses prior to the update.

Some new types of stone have been added: granite, diorite, and andesite. These stones are found when mining but can also be crafted with specific recipes. All three can be crafted into smooth versions, much like cobblestone, but cannot be crafted into stairs or slabs.

Glass

Glass is made by smelting sand in a furnace. Once you have glass blocks, you can craft panes of glass from them on your crafting bench (**Figure 4.6**). Glass can be dyed one of 16 colors, making stained glass. If you want to have colored panes of glass, you need to dye the blocks first and then make the glass panes.

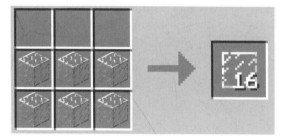

FIGURE 4.6 Glass pane recipe: six glass blocks (of any color).

Clay

Clay (**Figure 4.7**) is found in riverbeds and on the ocean floor. Unless your shovel has a Silk Touch enchant, you will get balls of clay that you can craft back into blocks.

FIGURE 4.7 From left to right: clay ball, clay block, hardened clay, clay brick, brick block, brick slab, brick stairs, and flower pot.

You can smelt clay balls into clay bricks, which you can then craft into brick blocks. Brick blocks can be crafted into stairs and slabs and are often used as a main building material for houses, foundations, roofs, and fireplaces. Clay bricks are also used to make flower pots.

If you use unsmelted clay balls to form clay blocks, the blocks can be hardened in a furnace and then dyed. Because hardened clay has a reddish tone, when it is dyed the result will also be more reddish. For instance, any blue dyes will become more purple when put on hardened clay. We'll look at dyeing clay in the "Dye" section.

Ores

Ores are the minerals in the game, like coal, iron, redstone, and diamond (**Figure 4.8**). There are two types of ore: those that need to be smelted, like iron and gold, and those that shatter into pieces when mined, like coal, redstone, lapis lazuli, emerald, diamond, and nether quartz. When you smelt gold or iron, the bars are called ingots, and they can be crafted into blocks by placing nine ingots on a crafting bench.

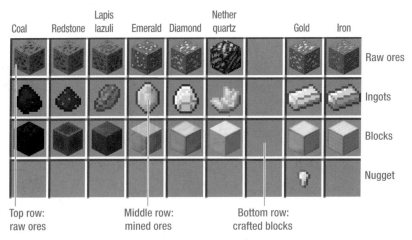

FIGURE 4.8 Ores in their raw, mined, smelted, and crafted forms.

When you are mining these ores, you should use the correct pick. Although you can use a stone pick to mine coal, lapis lazuli, iron, and nether quartz, you can't mine redstone, gold, emeralds, and diamonds with anything weaker than an iron pick. A diamond pick is the strongest, and you'll need fewer hits to break the ore. Enchanted tools are the best, as a Silk Touch enchant allows you to mine ores and blocks without altering their original form, and Fortune will cause blocks you mine to drop more of the ores. These can't be applied to the same tool, but they can be enchanted alongside an Unbreaking enchantment, which makes gear last longer, or an Efficiency enchant, which helps you mine more blocks in less time.

Other Building Blocks

Many other types of block exist. Some are found in the Overworld, like wool, obsidian, ice, and packed ice, while others require you to travel to other dimensions. You can find end stone only in the End, and you can find glowstone, soul sand, and netherrack only in the Nether. You can even use some food blocks, like pumpkins and melons, for building.

- Wool is harvested from sheep. You'll get one block of wool when you kill a sheep, whereas shearing them will cause the sheep to drop one to three blocks, and they will regrow their wool if they have grass to eat.

  You can dye blocks of wool or an entire sheep one of 16 colors. It takes one dye per wool block or one dye per sheep, and since sheep can be shorn repeatedly, it makes more sense to dye the sheep than the individual pieces of wool. Sheep and wool can be re-dyed another color as well.

  Dyed wool can be crafted into carpets or used to craft banners.

- Ice is found in snowy biomes and can be harvested with a pick. It is slippery, so when you run on it you can move faster. You can use it to move items more quickly in harvesters. Ice melts when there are torches close by.

- Packed ice is found only in the hard-to-find Ice Plains Spikes biomes. It doesn't melt, making it a better building block than ice.

- Obsidian is a deep black, hard stone that can be mined only with a diamond pick. It is formed when lava and water meet. It can also be found in pillars in the End. Obsidian is the hardest minable block in Minecraft (bedrock can't be mined in survival games) and is useful when making explosive-proof defenses.

  You need obsidian to make Nether portals, which you form by making a minimum 4x5 obsidian frame and lighting the inside.

- Prismarine occurs in ocean monuments, a new structure introduced with the 1.8 version update. Prismarine, prismarine brick, and dark prismarine, along with glowing sea lanterns, are new blocks that you can mine in the monuments. You can also craft them from prismarine shards and crystals, which are dropped by the guardian mob, a fish that lives in and near the ocean monuments.

- Nether blocks occur in the Nether (**Figure 4.9**). Most of the Nether is formed of netherrack, which is easy to mine (and lava, which is easy to fall into). With care, though, you can quickly collect netherrack, which can be smelted to form nether bricks. Nether bricks can be crafted into nether brick blocks, and from there into slabs and stairs.

Soul sand, nether wart, nether quartz or, nether quartz

Quartz block, chiseled quartz, pillar quartz, quartz slab, quartz stairs

Netherrack, nether brick, nether brick block, nether brick slab, nether brick stair

FIGURE 4.9 Blocks, ores, and items found in the Nether.

You will find nether quartz mixed in with the netherrack. It can be collected like the other ores and crafted into quartz blocks, which can be used to make chiseled and pillar quartz blocks as well as slabs and stairs.

Soul sand is found in patches throughout the Nether and has the unique property of slowing you or mobs down when it is walked on. When placed in water or on ice, the effects are magnified, making it useful for traps. It is also the only block that you can grow nether wart on.

Dye

Dyes are crafted from various items found in the game: flowers, squid ink sacs, mined lapis lazuli gems, and harvested cocoa beans and cactus.

Dyes come in 16 colors. You use them to color wool, glass, clay, and leather armor. You also use dye to color firework stars, craft banners, and change the color of a dog's collar.

Crafting Dye

To craft the dye, you simply put the dye ingredient into a crafting grid and collect the dye. These are shapeless recipes—you can place the ingredient anywhere in the grid. Most dyes are craftable with a single ingredient, and may have more than one recipe (**Figure 4.10**), but a few need to be made by combining two dyes (**Figure 4.11**).

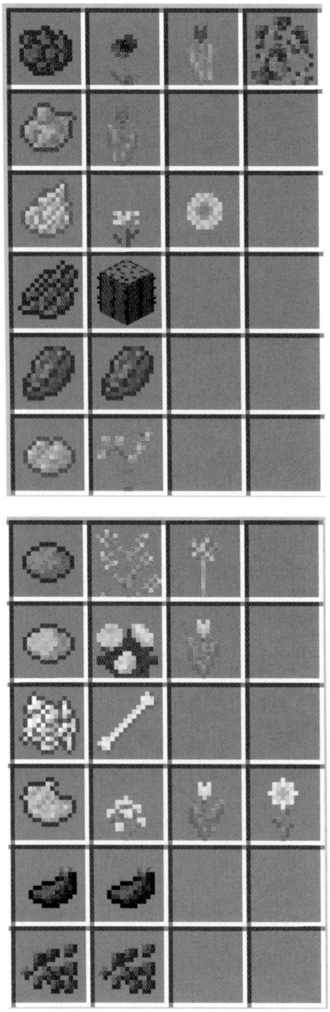

Red: poppy, red tulip, rosebush

Orange: orange tulip

Yellow: dandelion, sunflower

Green: cactus (must be cooked in furnace)

Blue: lapis lazuli (doesn't need to be crafted before use)

Light blue: blue orchid

Magenta: lilac, allium

Pink: peony, pink tulip

White: bonemeal (crafted from bones)

Light gray: Azure bluet, white tulip, oxeye daisy

Black: ink sac (doesn't need to be crafted before use)

Brown: cocoa beans (doesn't need to be crafted before use)

FIGURE 4.10 Many dyes can be crafted from a single ingredient, and often there is more than one way to craft them.

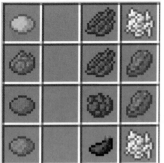

Lime green: combine green dye and bonemeal

Cyan: combine green dye and lapis lazuli

Purple: combine red dye and lapis lazuli

Gray: combine ink sac and bonemeal

FIGURE 4.11 These dyes need to be crafted by combining two dyes on a crafting bench.

Dyeing Wool, Clay, and Glass

When dyeing wool, you need one piece of dye for each block of wool, and you can just drop the dye and wool in the crafting bench. To color carpets, you need to dye the wool blocks before crafting them into carpets.

When you are dyeing (or staining) blocks of glass or hardened clay, however, you place one piece of dye in the center of the crafting grid, surrounded by eight blocks of glass or clay (**Figure 4.12**). As with the wool, if you'd like stained glass panes instead of blocks, you must dye the blocks before crafting the panes.

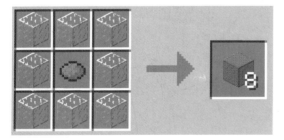

FIGURE 4.12 Stained glass or clay recipe: place 8 blocks around the dye.

Even though the dye is the same, the effects are different for wool, clay, and glass due to the nature of the materials being dyed. The transparency of the glass changes the vibrancy of the colors, and the red tone of hardened clay is blended with the dyes, changing the resulting color (**Figure 4.13**).

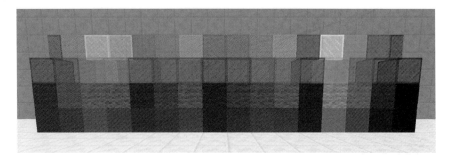

FIGURE 4.13 From top to bottom: Stained glass panes, stained glass blocks, dyed wool, stained clay.

Dyeing Leather Armor

You can dye leather armor, but unlike any of the other methods of dyeing, you can combine dyes, both on the crafting bench or by adding colors to previously dyed armor (**Figure 4.14**). Thanks to the many color choices, you have millions of tones and shades to choose from, and it can be great fun to play with the options.

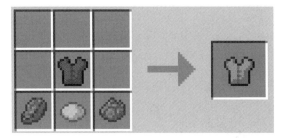

FIGURE 4.14 When dyeing leather, you can combine dyes to make unique color combinations.

Banners

Crafted from wool and sticks, banners are an exciting new decoration that can be hung on walls or placed on the floor. You can use dyes and items like vines, mob heads, and golden apples to create virtually endless and unique designs.

You can create patterns on a banner by placing the banner and the dye or other items in specific places on a crafting bench. You can layer up to six designs, wash them off one layer at a time in a cauldron, and copy them using a blank banner.

You can craft lots of patterns, including stripes, borders, shapes, and symbols. Experiment with them and check the wiki for basic recipes. **Figure 4.15** shows you the basic banner pattern with three patterns layered over it.

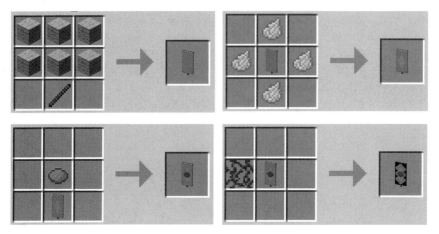

FIGURE 4.15 A basic banner recipe: 6 wool blocks, stick (top left), 4 pieces of dye around the banner for a diamond (top right), a single dye above the banner for a circle (bottom left), and vines beside the banner for a wavy border (bottom right).

Tools and Gear

Basic tools and gear will be some of the first things you'll craft. The main tools are the pickaxe, shovel, hoe, and axe (**Figure 4.16**), but tools like flint and steel, shears, fishing rods, and leads will come in handy as well.

Use your crafting bench to make your tools, using wooden sticks to make the handles and using wood, stone, gold, iron, or diamond for the heads.

The materials you choose (or have available) will affect how well your tool works and how long it will last. Some ores need an iron or diamond tool to be mined. When you start to use a tool (and this applies to armor as well), a meter will appear on the tool in your inventory, showing its durability.

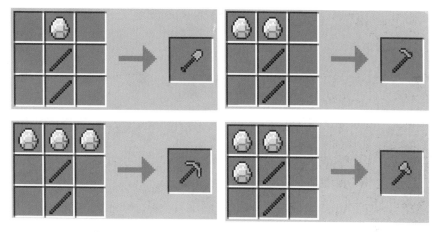

FIGURE 4.16 Basic tools: shovel, hoe, pickaxe, and axe here are made from diamond, although they can be crafted from wood, stone, gold, or iron as well.

Wooden tools are the least durable, diamond tools the most. Stone tools are great for starting out or for quick jobs, but they're not strong enough to mine all blocks. Gold, while pretty, is soft and will wear out quickly. Iron is a strong material that is less costly than diamonds, making it a good choice for basic tools until you've mined enough diamond (which you can only do with iron or diamond tools). If you use a tool on a block that it isn't suited for, such as cutting trees with a pick, it will take you longer and the tool will wear out faster.

Tools can be enchanted on an enchanting table by using experience points or by using an enchanted book with an anvil. They add specific bonus properties to your gear. If you put an Unbreaking enchantment on a tool, for example, it will last longer. You can repair and name tools on an anvil, but this takes both experience points and more of the material you use to craft your tool. When you name items, the name shows in your inventory. Named weapons show in death messages if you use them to kill an opponent. Because of the cost in experience points, you might want to use your enchantments for iron or diamond tools, which have the best endurance.

Tools have varying levels of efficacy, such as how many hits it takes to break a block. Diamond and iron are more efficient than wood, stone, or gold, meaning it takes fewer hits to break the block. You can get an Efficiency enchantment that means it will take fewer hits to break blocks, letting you work faster.

You will likely want to make other tools and items such as buckets, shears, and leads.

- Buckets can be used to carry water, lava, and milk and are incredibly useful tools (**Figure 4.17**). You'll need a bucket to carry water for a farm, though a bucket of water in your hotbar (your main inventory, which shows at the bottom of your screen) can be a lifesaver when you are mining or exploring lava-filled caves. A bucket of milk can save your life if you are attacked by poisonous cave spiders or encounter a potion-throwing witch, because drinking milk is an antidote for their poison.

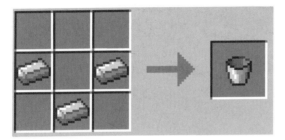

FIGURE 4.17 Bucket recipe: 3 iron ingots.

- Shears are needed to shear sheep, giving you more wool than if you kill the sheep (**Figure 4.18**). You can also use shears on trees, which will give you leaf blocks, as opposed to cutting down the trees, which will result in the leaf blocks disintegrating. Shears are also helpful with cobwebs, turning them to string, and if you put a Silk Touch enchantment on shears with an enchanted book, you can use shears to collect cobwebs without breaking them.

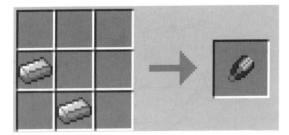

FIGURE 4.18 Shears recipe: 2 iron ingots.

Leads are great tools for moving and containing mobs (**Figure 4.19**). By right-clicking the animal with the lead in your hand, you'll attach it and be able to pull it along. Right-click again on a fence and the lead will be tied to it. You can lead more than one animal at a time, each on a separate lead. While you're riding a horse or donkey, you can use a lead to bring a second horse or donkey along.

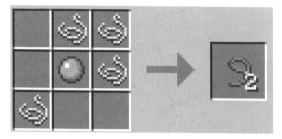

FIGURE 4.19 Lead recipe: 1 green slime ball and 4 pieces of string.

Flint and steel are used to start fires (**Figure 4.20**), but be careful, because trees and wooden houses are flammable, and it would be sad to see everything go up in flames. This is a handy tool for lighting Nether portals. Flint and steel can also occasionally be found in dungeon and fortress chests.

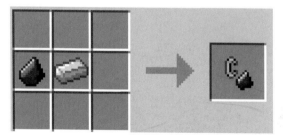

FIGURE 4.20 Flint and steel: flint and iron ingot.

Fishing rods are useful tools (**Figure 4.21**). Not only can you use them to catch fish (a good food source and needed to tame ocelots into cats), but you can also "catch" other items when you are fishing. The list of items you can catch is lengthy and divided into treasure and junk by Mojang. Some of the treasures include rare, uncraftable saddles and nametags, enchanted books, and fishing rods. Some of the junk includes useful items like leather, bottles, and ink sacs, though you might just catch boots (old, used, and without enchantments) or rotten flesh. You can enchant fishing rods with Lure or Luck of the Sea enchantments, which will speed up your fishing and increase your odds of getting a good catch.

If you craft a fishing rod with a carrot, you'll get a carrot on a stick, which is needed if you want to saddle up a pig and go for a ride.

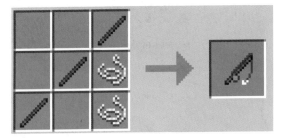

FIGURE 4.21 Fishing rod recipe: three wood sticks and two pieces of string.

Weapons and Armor

Weapons and armor are necessary tools if you're playing a survival game, and fun to play with even in Creative mode.

Weapons

Swords (**Figure 4.22**), needed for defense from hostile mobs and to hunt animals for food, are crafted with a wooden stick for a handle, and wood, stone, gold, iron, or diamond for the blade (Figure 4.22). The properties are the same as for tools—iron and diamond last longer and are better than wood, stone, or gold.

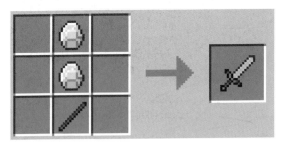

FIGURE 4.22 Sword recipe: one wood stick and two diamonds (also craftable from wood, stone, gold, and iron).

Bows and arrows can be crafted or collected from skeletons (**Figure 4.23**).

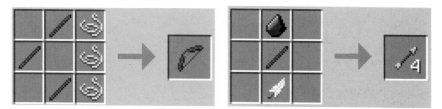

FIGURE 4.23 Bow recipe: three sticks and three pieces of string (left); arrow recipe: flint, stick, feather (right).

Armor

There are four different pieces of armor: helmet, chest or chest plate, leggings, and boots (**Figure 4.24**). You can make armor from leather, gold, iron, and diamond, and they will have the same relative durability as tools made from each material. You can also enchant armor with various enchantments. Like tools, armor wears out and will need to be repaired or replaced. New with the 1.8 update, you also can craft an armor stand to hold your armor, mob heads, and pumpkins.

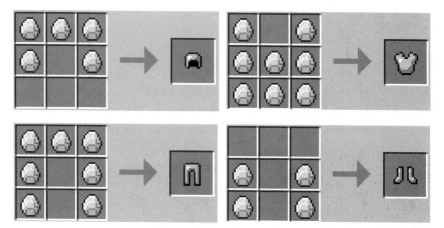

FIGURE 4.24 Helmet recipe: five diamonds; chest plate recipe: eight diamonds; leggings recipe: seven diamonds; boots recipe: four diamonds. Armor can also be crafted with the same recipes using leather, gold, or iron ingots.

Enchanting

Enchanting is a complex part of the game, and one that has changed with the 1.8 update. You can enchant tools, weapons, and books on a specially crafted enchanting table, and different items have different enhancements (**Figure 4.25**). Enchanting will cost you experience points (XP), and as of the 1.8 update, they will also cost you up to three lapis lazuli.

You can enchant books yourself, find them in chests in dungeons, or catch them when fishing. You can also use an anvil to combine enchants, or to add them to an item from an enchanted book. Village priests sometimes exchange enchanted items in trade for emeralds or other goods.

FIGURE 4.25 An enchanting table allows you to place a variety of enchantments on your items.

Enchanting is done on an enchanting table, which you can craft with diamonds, obsidian, and a book (**Figure 4.26**). You can increase the level of enchants that are available by surrounding your enchanting table with bookcases. For instance, at a table without shelves, you may enchant items costing only a couple of experience points, but as you add bookcases (up to 15 within a 5x5 square and not directly touching the enchanting table), your table will become more powerful, allowing you to use up to 30 experience points on one enchant. You have a higher chance of getting a good enchant when the XP cost is higher.

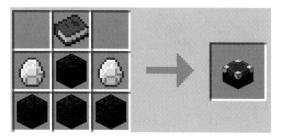

FIGURE 4.26 Enchanting table recipe: one book, two diamonds, and four obsidian blocks.

The new enchanting system also will cost you lapis lazuli, though it requires fewer XP. You have a choice of three enchants, depending on how many pieces of lapis you use, and you'll get a sneak peek at one of the enchants you'll receive, something that wasn't possible in earlier versions of the game (**Figure 4.27**).

FIGURE 4.27 The enchanting table menu. Here, I'm using two lapis lazuli, so only the top two enchants are available. Hovering over the second shows me I'll get an Unbreaking II enchant at a cost of 12 XP (when I did enchant the sword, the second enchant was a Smite II).

Enchants are specific to the item. For instance, you may get an Infinity enchant on a bow, which allows you to carry only one arrow but never run out, but you wouldn't get it on a pair of boots, on which you might get a Protection or Feather Falling enchant.

Enchanted books often have a combination of enchants that are unique to certain tools or items. You use an anvil to put the enchants on the item of your choice, but only the enchants that fit that item will be applied to it.

Experience Points

You collect experience points by mining ores, smelting items in a furnace, killing mobs (including friendly mobs like cows and pigs), and breeding animals. If you die, you lose your experience points.

You can gain experience points much faster by building a mob grinder, which makes use of one or more mob spawners to collect mobs. Usually a mechanism is created within the grinder that will weaken them so that they are easily killed. They may spawn above water, which will move them toward a chute and cause them to fall and take damage. You can then finish them off easily and collect the experience points. You can easily find designs for spawners online.

Anvil

An anvil is used to repair and name gear, to combine enchants from various tools, and to apply enchants from books to gear. Like the enchanting table, all these actions cost experience points. You craft an anvil with iron bars and blocks (**Figure 4.28**).

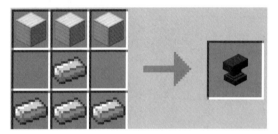

FIGURE 4.28 Anvil recipe: three iron blocks and four iron ingots.

To use an anvil, right-click it, and then place the item to be repaired in the first box. In the second box, place a second one of the same item, an enchanted book (**Figure 4.29**), or raw materials. You will be told how many experience points the repair will cost, and you see from the bar on the item whether it will be fully or partially repaired. The repair is finished when you pick up the item. When you combine two enchanted items, the enchantments are combined on the repaired item. Anvils take damage when used and will eventually break.

FIGURE 4.29 Using an anvil to add an enchant to an item, such as this Luck of the Sea enchant on a fishing rod, costs experience points and will cause the enchanted item to glow. Here, I've renamed the fishing rod while enchanting it.

Transportation

When you start a new map, chances are you'll do a lot of walking, but soon enough you might find that you've run out of land, or just that you'd like to hit the water in your own little boat. Once you've gathered enough materials or stumbled upon an abandoned mineshaft, you may want to set up rail lines too. And let's not forget that you can now travel by horse. There are many more ways to traverse the map than simply on foot. You can find information on horses in the "Mobs" section, but let's take a quick look at boats and rail.

Boats

Traveling by boat is how I prefer to start exploring a map, particularly if I am on a server with others and might want to get away from my spawn point before I settle but don't have many resources yet. I often find friendly mobs along the shore, and sometimes bump into a village. When you're traveling by boat, your hunger bar disappears and you won't need to eat. This is helpful when you're starting out—you can head to the sea at night, avoid mobs, not need food, and explore the coast line.

All you need to make a boat is five planks, which is easy even when you're just starting out (**Figure 4.30**). Boats break exceptionally easily, dropping planks and sticks—and you. It is wise to make and carry a few boats, or at least carry some extra planks or logs to make more.

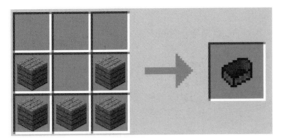

FIGURE 4.30 Boat recipe: five planks.

You place a boat by right-clicking it, then right-clicking again to get in. To move, use W to move forward while steering with your mouse. Move backward with the S key. Be careful to avoid land and obstacles when you're in your boat or it might break. To get out (presuming it didn't break when you arrived ashore), Shift-click.

Minecarts

Minecarts, like boats, can be ridden, and you use the same mechanics for getting in and out of the cart. Although you are restricted to traveling only where rails have been laid, carts are much faster than walking, and they can be used to transport mobs and items (**Figure 4.31**). To get moving in a cart, you need to start your minecart on a slope or get a push, unless you use powered rails and a button to launch you. Once in motion, you will slow down pretty quickly unless you use a powered minecart or powered rails to propel you.

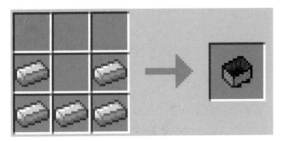

FIGURE 4.31 Minecart recipe: five iron ingots.

Once you make a minecart, you can combine it on a crafting bench with a furnace, a chest, a hopper, TNT, a mob spawner, or a command block to create specialized carts (**Figure 4.32**).

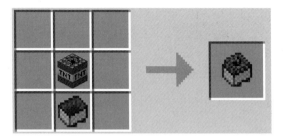

FIGURE 4.32 You can add items to a minecart.

You can make a powered minecart that carries a furnace filled with coal, and this can be placed alongside other minecarts to make a train. Powered minecarts can only push the other cars, not pull them, so you need to place it at the back of the train, or place one at either end. To start your minecart, right-click it with your fuel (coal or charcoal) while facing the direction you'd like it to move.

Adding a chest to a minecart allows you to use it for storage or to transport items. If you put a hopper on a minecart, it will collect items on or just above the track. The amount of material that a chest or hopper is holding will change how far the cart will go using powered tracks; a full cart will need more powered tracks to keep it running.

A TNT minecart will activate and explode just as TNT does. It will explode if it drops more than three blocks at the end of a track, if it crosses an activator rail (there is a delay before it explodes), if it hits lava or water, or if it is hit by something while it is moving. Be careful when you're playing with TNT, because the explosion will cause damage to you and the surrounding area.

Rails

Tracks, or rails, are easily crafted with iron and a stick (**Figure 4.33**). You can also find them in abandoned mineshafts, where they are easy to collect with a pick. Tracks are needed for minecarts, but basic unpowered tracks won't help the cart move unless you use a powered minecart or add powered rails along the route.

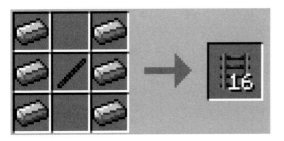

FIGURE 4.33 Minecart tracks or rails recipe: six iron ingots and a stick.

Powered rails (**Figure 4.34**) use redstone power to either propel trains (when they are on) or to stop them (acting as brakes when they are off). They need to be powered, usually with a lever or a redstone torch or block placed beside or under the powered rails, although they can be powered by detector rails as well.

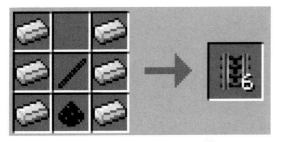

FIGURE 4.34 Powered rails recipe: six gold ingots, a stick, and redstone dust.

You can lay rails on your route in many ways, and there have been all sorts of experiments to see how hills, weight of the cars, number of cars, and other factors affect the speed and length of time the minecart will travel before it loses speed. A fairly agreed upon spacing is to have one powered rail for every 38 regular rails, although often people will place one after 25 or 30 rails. Feel free to experiment and look online to see what others have done. The Minecraft wiki is a great source for more information on rails, including activator rails, which activate TNT, hoppers, and command block carts, and detector rails, which provide power when weight crosses them.

You can use minecarts and tracks for transportation across distances, to transport many items at once, and for fun. Making elaborate rollercoasters can be a great challenge, and they are fun to ride.

Potions

Once you've been playing for a while and collected many items (and let's face it, Minecraft is a game for hoarders and collectors), you'll be ready to start looking at crafting potions.

Potions come in two forms: a drinkable version, and a splash potion that you can throw at others. Some provide personal benefits, like being able to move faster or become invisible, while others can be used defensively, such as a splash potion that will weaken or slow your enemies.

There are several steps to brewing potions, but before you begin any of them, you need to craft a brewing stand (**Figure 4.35**). A brewing stand is easy to craft, but its recipe needs a blaze rod, which you can only get from hunting a blaze in a Nether fortress—it might take you a while before you can get the blaze rod to craft the brewing station. You can place the brewing station on most block surfaces. Many players have brewing rooms where they gather all the materials they need to brew potions, as well as a cauldron or an endless water supply for filling bottles of water.

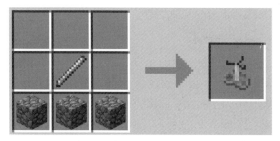

FIGURE 4.35 Brewing stand recipe: one blaze rod and three cobbleston.

Brewing potions requires several steps. We're going to make a Potion of Invisibility to illustrate the steps.

All potions except the Potion of Weakness start with an Awkward Potion for the base. For this we need glass bottles of water and nether wart, a plant that grows only on soul sand and is found in nether fortresses. You can craft the bottles from glass blocks (**Figure 4.36**).

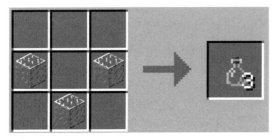

FIGURE 4.36 Glass bottle recipe: three glass blocks.

The brewing stand can brew three bottles of potion at a time, using a single ingredient that is divided between the three bottles, so it makes sense to always make three potions.

To make your Awkward Potion, fill your glass bottles with water by clicking them into an endless water source or a cauldron. Click the brewing stand to open it, and place your bottles of water in it. Add a piece of nether wart to the space at the top, and wait for your potion to brew (**Figure 4.37**).

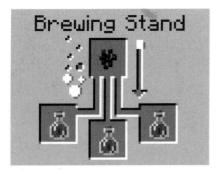

FIGURE 4.37 Adding nether wart to bottles of water in a brewing stand to make an awkward potion.

Once you have your base potion, you will add the next potion ingredient to the brewing stand. For some potions, this might be the final step, but in order to make a Potion of Invisibility, we need to first make a Potion of Night Vision. To do this, leave the bottles of Awkward Potion where they are and add a golden carrot (made by surrounding a carrot with golden nuggets on the crafting bench).

When the brewing is complete, you'll have a Potion of Night Vision that will last for three minutes.

Since we're making the Potion of Invisibility, we need to leave the bottles where they are and add a third ingredient. We need a fermented spider eye, which we craft by combining a brown mushroom, sugar, and a spider's eye on a crafting bench. Add the fermented spider's eye to the brewing stand, and wait for it to process. The wait times are short—you can have several stands brewing at once and by the time you're putting the ingredients in the last one, the first will be ready for the next step.

Once the brewing is complete, you will have three bottles of potion of invisibility, but they will only last for three minutes. For the very low cost of a piece of redstone dust, you can extend that to eight minutes. Leave the potions where they are and add the redstone.

Once you have your potions, remove them from the stand. To drink them, hold one in your inventory and right-click. If you want to turn these potions into splash potions, leave them in the brewing stand and add one final ingredient: gunpowder will turn any potion into a splash potion and can be added at any step.

As you can see, brewing can be a complex and complicated process, both in the ingredients needed and in the steps to take. Once you break the steps down, however, and remember that some things are the same no matter what potion you're brewing, it becomes much easier.

There are more potions than we have room to list here, but you can find the recipes for all of them online. Remember that almost all potions start with an Awkward Potion base. Most can be extended from three to eight minutes with redstone dust, or in some cases made more potent with glowstone dust, though redstone dust will cancel the effects of glowstone dust and vice versa. To make a splash potion, add gunpowder. The rest of the ingredients are unique to the potion, but are easily found online. Have fun brewing!

Fireworks

You can make over 900 different varieties of fireworks. With all those options and a bit of time and energy, you can put on an amazing fireworks show. Because quite a few of the parts are hard to come by, it is good to experiment with fireworks on a creative map, where you can use all the materials you want.

Fireworks are made from a firework rocket and a firework star. If you craft the rocket without adding the star, it will shoot but there won't be any explosives. Firework stars are crafted to contain dye (16 colors to choose from) and special effects items. You then craft your firework rocket, including the firework star (or stars, you can add more than one to a single firework rocket) and one, two, or three pieces of gunpowder, which will determine how high your firework will shoot (**Figure 4.38**).

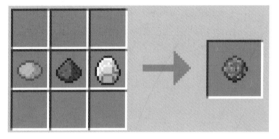

FIGURE 4.38 Lime green small firework star with a trail recipe: lime green dye, gunpowder, and a diamond.

To make a firework star, you need one piece of gunpowder and up to 8 colors of dye.

To design the shape of your firework, you can add one (and only one) of the following: a fire charge to make a large ball, a gold nugget for a star shape, a feather for a burst, or a creeper head for a creeper-head-shaped explosion. In addition, if you add a diamond, your firework will leave a trail, and if you add glowstone dust, it will sparkle.

Once you have made your firework star or stars, it is time to add them to your rockets. To make your firework rocket, you will need a piece of paper, up to three pieces of gunpowder (these determine height, remember), and one or more firework stars (**Figure 4.39**).

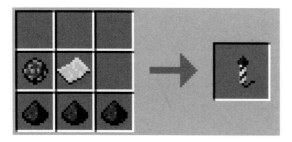

FIGURE 4.39 Recipe to craft a firework rocket: 1 piece of paper; 1, 2, or 3 pieces of gunpowder (to set the height); and up to 7 fireworks stars.

Go Crafting

This should give you a good taste of some of the ways that you craft items in Minecraft. There are many more, from foods to all sorts of blocks for building, and from books you can write in, to furniture for your house. Experiment with the various items, see what recipes you can discover, and devise new designs. Most of all, be creative and have fun!

The Lay of the Land

Just like the real world, Minecraft has many types of land. The different areas are called *biomes*, and each has unique features, such as certain plants, ores, or landscapes. Minecraft biomes are mostly divided by climate (snowy, cold, lush, dry, and so on), and each category has a variety of more specific biomes, for a total of 61 different types.

When you start a new map, the biomes are randomly generated, though in such a way that you won't find a hot desert next to a snowy mountain. They aren't very large, so you can travel from one to the other pretty quickly (**Figure 4.40**). When you're looking for cocoa beans and jungle wood and are in the middle of a desert, you are going to have to go exploring until you find a jungle biome. With relatively small biomes, chances are it won't take you very long.

Sometimes it is hard to tell which biome you are in. Press F3 to display a lot of information, including your coordinates, the direction you are facing, and your current biome.

Plains   River   Beach   Forest   Ocean   Tiaga

FIGURE 4.40 Here we see how small biomes intersect.

We'll look at the main features of each biome (**Figures 4.41** and **4.42**), but if you'd like more information, see the biomes page on the Minecraft wiki.

FIGURE 4.41 Three neighboring biomes. From left to right: plains, taiga, extreme hills.

FIGURE 4.42 Three more biomes: roofed forest, swamp, extreme hills.

Plains and Sunflower Plains

Plains are grassy flatlands, with small hills, scattered flowers, and the occasional tree. Many animals spawn on plains, including cows, sheep, and pigs. You'll also find horses and donkeys here. Sunflower plains are simply plains that also contain sunflowers.

You can find villages here that contain NPC (non-playable characters) that you can trade with.

Savannah

The savannah is rather like a dry, rain-free version of plains, although there is also the very mountainous Savannah M biome. The same animals, including horses and donkeys, spawn here, but the grass is more brown and dry. You can also find acacia trees in these biomes.

Forest

Many types of forest biomes exist. Although they share similar traits, the most obvious being that they are filled with trees, they have a lot of variety. In some, like regular and birch forests, you will find slight hills, a lot of grass, and many trees. Others are more hilly, have larger or taller trees, or in the case of roofed forests with dark oak, are much darker and more difficult to navigate. Hostile mobs can be common in forests, even during the day, because they may not be exposed to the sunlight that will cause them to despawn.

Flower forests have a higher number of flowers, including some that can't be found elsewhere.

Swamp

Swamps are wetlands that are found along the shore. They are often made of many small islands in shallow water and are a good place to collect sand, clay, and reeds. Slime spawns here, and you'll find witches' huts as well, so be careful!

Jungle

Jungle biomes are divided into two types: flat and more mountainous. Jungle edges are considered to be their own biome as well, with fewer trees. All jungle biomes feature thick forests with tall jungle wood trees (which produce cocoa beans) and vines. You can find jungle temples here. Jungles are the only place you'll be able to find ocelots, which you can tame to become pet cats by using fish.

Desert

Deserts are relatively large sand and sandstone biomes, filled with cactus, villages, and the occasional desert temple. You won't find friendly mobs like cows or pigs here, and most hostile mobs don't last once the sun rises, because there is no shade.

Mesa

Mesa and the Bryce mesa are less common biomes. They are hot and dry, made of layers of clay, and have red sand instead of regular sand. You'll find tall formations and columns in the Bryce mesa (**Figure 4.43**).

FIGURE 4.43 Desert biome in the foreground with mesa behind.

Taiga

Much like a forest but filled with spruce trees, ponds, and rivers, taiga biomes can be warm or frozen, and flat or mountainous. Common features are spruce trees and ferns. These are the only biomes that contain wolves, which can be tamed to become pet dogs.

Extreme Hills

Much like the name suggests, extreme hills biomes feature high and steep hills, mountains, and cliffs. Extreme hills biomes have snow at high elevations and are the only place to find emeralds.

Mushroom Island

Extremely rare, mushroom island biomes are covered in giant mushrooms. You'll find mycelium blocks in this biome. Mooshrooms (mushroom-covered red cows) spawn here, but no other mobs spawn naturally.

Ice Plains and Ice Plains Spikes

Another uncommon biome is the ice plains—large plains covered with snow and packed ice and little else. Ice Plains Spikes is a related biome that is very similar and has spikes of packed ice rising from the ground (**Figure 4.44**)

FIGURE 4.44 Ice Plains Spikes biome.

Rivers, Hills, Plateaus, Beaches, and Oceans

Many biomes don't have any distinctive features, but form a border between other biomes; they are a variation of major biomes.

Beaches and stone beaches occur along oceans and deep oceans. River biomes are simply rivers, often cutting between other biomes. Like swamps, they are a good place to collect clay and sand.

Biome Variations

Many biomes have several similar variations. Some are in hill or plateau form, which are exactly as they sound. You can find hilly savannah or mesa plateau, for instance.

One other variation in biomes is the climate—many biomes occur in warm, snowy, or icy versions. For example, you'll find regular plains and snow plains.

Combining all these variations along with the biomes results in 61 different biomes.

Nether

The Nether is more than simply another biome—it's more of a world-sized dimension. You can access it only through a Nether portal. The Nether has its own map and is completely underground, with no sky, no night and day, and no weather. Water evaporates here, but there are many seas formed of lava (**Figure 4.45**).

FIGURE 4.45 The lava-full Nether.

Many blocks and mobs are unique to the Nether. The blocks include netherrack, quartz, glowstone, and soul sand. Mobs that are unique to the Nether include magma cubes, ghasts, blazes, wither skeletons, and zombie pigmen. Nether fortresses, which are large dungeons, are located here.

To access the Nether, you will need to build a Nether portal by making a frame out of obsidian (though the corners can be any material). Your frame needs to be at least four blocks wide and five blocks high, but it can be as large as 23 blocks on each side. To activate the portal, light the inside of the frame with lava, flint and steel, or by using a fire charge. The center will fill with swirling purple light. Step into the opening and you'll be transported to the Nether (**Figure 4.46**).

FIGURE 4.46 A nether portal.

Nether portals, also known as gates, can be complicated, as moving one block in the Nether is the same as moving eight blocks in the Overworld. This means that portals can sometimes overlap—while you take one portal to get to the Nether, you may end up somewhere different on the trip home, but it also means that you can make and use Nether portals to help you travel great distances in less time.

Sky/End

The Sky, or End, is a dark, bare dimension that you can access only through an end portal, which occurs only in a rare, difficult-to-find stronghold. The End is the only place to find and fight the Ender Dragon, the main (and pretty much only) boss fight in Minecraft. You'll also find End stone here, as well as many, many endermen (**Figure 4.47**).

FIGURE 4.47 The End, complete with Ender Dragon.

World-Generated Structures

Landscapes on Minecraft maps are formed with world-generated structures, from lakes and ravines to villages and dungeons (**Figure 4.48**). These structures shape and add detail to the world.

Many don't require any discussion, but it is interesting to think that even something as simple as trees, glowstone, a spring of water, a lava pool, or the ores you mine are programmed to generate at certain locations and with specific frequency. Ravines and caverns are great for caving, a mining technique that takes advantage of the open walls that expose ores. Features such as ice spikes, mossy stone boulders, and giant mushrooms offer a decorative touch.

Other world-generated structures, however, are much larger and add to the gameplay. Villages, fortresses, and abandoned mineshafts fall into this category and deserve a closer look.

FIGURE 4.45 World-generated structures, clockwise from upper left: abandoned mineshaft in a ravine, blaze spawner in a Nether fortress, jungle temple, End portal in a stronghold, village and desert temple, ocean monument.

Villages

Villages are collections of houses and gardens populated by villagers. They occur in plains, savannah, and desert biomes. They can make a great home base or provide materials in the form of food from the gardens, treasure from a chest (usually found in the blacksmith's house), and items in the houses them-selves, such as bookshelves and furnaces. Villagers are non-player characters (NPCs) that will trade with players, using emeralds and other items for currency.

Dungeons

Encased in mossy cobblestone, dungeons often occur in abandoned mine-shafts and are scattered underground across the map. They contain a monster spawner (skeleton, zombie, or spider) and chests with treasure. You can stop the monsters from spawning by placing a torch on the spawner (or, if you're as paranoid as me, many torches).

Desert and Jungle Temples

Temples in deserts and jungles offer treasures—and traps. Desert temples have a hidden pit in the middle, filled with chests... and also with a pressure plate that will set off TNT if touched. Jungle temples have a puzzle of levers as well as a tripwire passageway to navigate.

Temples are worth exploring—not only do they provide a fun challenge, but they are among the few places you can find treasures that can't be crafted, such as iron, gold, and diamond horse armor.

Ocean Monument

One of the newest additions to Minecraft is the ocean monument. While it's not a source of treasure chests, you can find special new blocks like prismarine and sea lanterns in these deep ocean structures, as well as new mobs like guardians and elder guardians.

Abandoned Mineshafts

Deep underground you'll occasionally discover abandoned mineshafts, usually cutting through ravines and caverns. These multi-story maze-like constructions are made from wood, with rail tracks running through them. Here, you'll find chests and minecart chests with treasures, and also venomous, deadly cave spider spawners.

Abandoned mineshafts are great for gathering wood, fence posts, treasure, ore from the walls, and rails, but they are also easy to get lost in and can be deadly. It is important to mark your path or use a map marker, and to explore them only when you are well prepared.

Strongholds

Strongholds are special fortresses that hold the End portal. No more than three spawn on a world, and they are underground and hard to find. You can craft an Eye of Ender from ender pearls and use it to locate strongholds by throwing it and following its path. Strongholds are much more designed than other structures, with prison cells, storage rooms, libraries, scattered chests of treasure, and of course the End portal.

Nether Fortresses

Deep in the Nether are fortresses made of netherbrick. You can find chests with semi-rare treasure tucked throughout the fortress. Only in Nether fortresses will you find blaze spawners and the nether wart plants. Nether fortresses are populated by wither skeletons and zombie pigmen.

Critters and Creatures

One of the most important parts of Minecraft is the mobs. From taking down exploding creepers to riding horses across the plains, mobs are a huge part of the game.

Types of Mobs

Mob is short for "mobile entity," meaning creatures that can move around the game. Each mob in Minecraft has specific characteristics. Some spawn in specific biomes or areas, or only at night or in a dark place, for instance.

Friendly mobs like cows, sheep, and horses are sometimes called *critters*. We use them for our farms and even keep some as pets. Other mobs, like endermen and creepers, we call *monsters* or *hostile mobs*. A few mobs are considered neutral. They won't hurt you unless you attack them, or even hit them accidentally. Then they become hostile mobs and will attack. Wolves are a great example of a mob that can go from neutral to friendly (if you tame them) or to hostile (if you hit them).

Villagers spawn only in villages, and you can trade items or emeralds with them for other items. They are susceptible to zombies, and they can become hostile zombie villagers when attacked.

Mob Spawning

Spawning is the word used to describe what happens when mobs pop into existence in the game. Friendly mobs can spawn at any time of day or night, but most hostile mobs spawn only at night or in places with low light. Some mobs have special spawning rules; when you kill a zombie, more will spawn immediately in the area, for example.

Light an area to stop mobs from spawning. Torches or lamps prevent the monsters from showing up. When daylight comes, most hostile mobs will catch fire and burn up, though they are still hostile and will attack even while they're on fire. Spiders stick around even during the day, but they attack only at night or in the dark.

Not only do mobs spawn randomly, but there are mob spawners in the game, often in dungeons and abandoned mineshafts; they cause a specific type of mob to spawn. These can be deactivated by placing torches on or beside the spawner, or they can be broken. Spawners can be used to make *grinders*, a place where mob spawns are controlled so that players can kill many in a safe manner in order to get experience points in a relatively short time (known as *grinding*).

Mob Drops

When mobs are killed, they leave behind items: meat, leather, or wool in the case of friendly mobs, and spider webs, rotten flesh, or weapons in the case of hostile monsters. These are known as *mob drops*, and each mob has specific drops. Many drop two or three different items, though not at the same time.

All mobs can be killed, but some are harder to kill than others. Use a sword or a bow and arrow for hunting or self-defense. Iron and diamond make the strongest swords, and enchanted weapons are even more effective, such as using a sword with a Looting enchantment, which will cause the mob to drop more items. When killed, mobs also leave behind green orbs, which are experience points that you can collect and are needed for enchantments.

Taming Mobs

Friendly mobs are very helpful in the game. Raising them in farms means you can have an easy supply of chicken, beef, pork, or wool. Most mobs are passive—you can lead them with food or on a lead and you can breed them, but that is the extent of interactions with them.

When you feed fish to ocelots or bones to wolves, you can tame them, turning them into pet cats and dogs. Sometimes this takes patience and a few tries, but once tamed the animals will follow you.

Horses can also be trained and ridden. You tame a horse by riding it. It might kick you off a few times, but keep trying—eventually it will show hearts and will be tamed. Unlike cats and dogs, horses aren't connected to one player after being tamed—others can ride them too.

Most of the friendly mobs can be bred to make babies by feeding two of them a certain item, such as wheat or carrots. The two animals will touch each other, and when they part there will be a baby between them; the player gets experience points. This is a good way to raise animals to farm.

Friendly Mobs

You will find friendly mobs in various biomes—most farm animals are found in plains, forests, taiga, and mountainous areas. If you want to put them in a pen or barn to farm them, they can be led with a lead or will follow food.

Cows

Drops: Leather; raw beef; milk (when touched with an empty bucket; doesn't kill the cow)

Breeding: Wheat

Cows spawn in plains and other grassy areas. They are very versatile and great to have in a farm. You can cook the beef they drop (or eat it raw, but you won't get as many hunger bars filled), and you can use the leather for making armor, books, and item frames.

Mooshrooms

Drops: Leather; raw beef; milk (when touched with an empty bucket; doesn't kill the mooshroom); mushroom stew (when tapped with a wooden bowl; doesn't harm the creature); mushrooms when sheared, although this turns them into a cow

Breeding: Wheat

Mooshrooms are hard to find, spawning only on the rare Mooshroom Island biome. They are even more versatile than cows, as they also provide stew.

Sheep

Drops: Wool, 1 block when killed, 1–3 when sheared, which grows back; mutton (version 1.8 and higher)

Breeding: Wheat

Sheep are useful as a source of wool and, as of version 1.8, as a source of food in the form of raw mutton. They are found in grassy areas such as plains and forests.

If you shear a sheep, it will drop up to three blocks of wool, which will grow back when they eat grass. They spawn in white, brown, black, gray, light gray, and occasionally pink, but they can be dyed any of the 16 colors by clicking them with a dye (the dye is then used up). See the section "Dye" for more information.

Pigs

Drops: Raw pork

Breed: Carrots

Pigs, found in grassy areas, are a source of pork but otherwise aren't very useful. They can be ridden by placing a saddle on them and then guiding them with a carrot on a stick, which you make by adding a carrot to a fishing rod on a crafting bench.

Pigs can be hit by lightning, turning them into zombie pigmen, although this is a rare occurrence.

Chickens

Drops: Eggs; raw chicken and feathers when killed

Breeding: Seeds. You can also hatch chicks by throwing eggs, although it can take many eggs to hatch a single chick.

Chickens are versatile farm animals. They lay eggs and drop raw chicken and feathers when they are killed, and you can use their eggs to make cakes and pies and their feathers to craft arrows and quill pens.

Rabbits

Drops: Hide; meat; rabbit's foot (rare)

Breeding: Carrots; golden carrots; dandelions

New as of version 1.8, rabbits come in six colors. They appear in almost all the biomes, and are, for the most part, a passive mob. A rabbit's foot can be used in potions.

Every so often, the very rare Killer Bunny will spawn. It is not shy like its brethren, and will attack players and cause a fair amount of damage. It will also attack wolves and pet dogs, so be careful!

Horses, Donkeys, and Mules

Drops: Leather, though horses are not typically bred for drops

Breeding: Golden carrots; golden apples (craft by surrounding a carrot or apple with gold nuggets in a crafting bench). You can breed two horses, two donkeys, or a horse and a donkey, which will produce a mule (mules cannot be bred).

Horses, donkeys, and mules spawn on the plains. Horses appear in many colors and patterns, which are combined to a total of 35 different versions. They each have specific characteristics in terms of jumping height and speed. They can be ridden, but only if you have a saddle, which cannot be crafted. You must find a saddle in dungeons and temple chests or by trading with villagers. You can also find iron, gold, and diamond horse armor; diamond horse armor cannot be crafted—you must find it.

You can ride donkeys and mules, and they will also carry a chest, something a horse cannot do. If you use a lead, you can ride a horse and pull a donkey carrying a chest behind you.

To tame a horse, you need to ride it (right-click to mount; Shift-click to dismount). This can take a few tries because you will likely be thrown and will need to remount. When you see floating hearts around the horse and it has calmed, it is tamed. Now you can ride and breed your horse.

Horses can eat many foods, including sugar, apples, carrots, bread, wheat, and hay. Unlike other mobs, they have inventory slots for their armor and saddle, and their own health meter.

Squid

Drops: Ink sacs

Breeding: Cannot be bred

Squid spawn in bodies of water. They provide ink sacs, which are used as a dye source and for writing books, making them valuable. They have no other purpose.

Ocelots/cats

Drops: None

Breeding: Raw fish

Ocelots are shy wild cats that spawn only in jungles. They don't like people, so it can take a bit of time and patience and a large supply of raw fish to tame them. Once tamed they turn into tabby, Siamese, or black and white tuxedo cats, which will follow you and teleport to be with you.

You can make your tamed cats stay safe by right-clicking them, which will seat them until you release them; this will keep from walking into fire, lava, or cactus and dying. On the other hand, since creepers avoid cats, it's not a bad idea to have some around when you're working at night or in dark spaces.

Cats are mischievous and like to sit on your furniture and sometimes run through your crops (kittens especially will do this). This can be frustrating if they're on your chests, preventing you from opening them, but you can lure them away with fish.

Bats

Drops: None

Breeding: Cannot be bred

Bats spawn in caves, and while they are cute, they have nothing to offer. They don't drop anything, but they won't attack either.

Villagers

Drops: None

Breeding: Villagers breed on their own, as long as they have enough buildings with doors

NPC villagers (sometimes called *testificates*) appear in villages. You can trade with them for goods. Villagers wear clothes that identify their job, such as priest, farmer, and librarian. Each villager starts out with one item they will trade, and when you make a trade, a new item is added to the options. Some trades may not seem fair, but you won't be able to open other trade options without making the exchange.

Villagers are favorite targets of zombies, and can become zombie villagers if they are attacked. They hide in their houses at night, and need doors so that they can seek safety and protect themselves.

Neutral Mobs

There are a few mobs that are friendly until they've been attacked, but which then turn fiercely hostile. Use care around these neutral mobs.

Wolves/dogs

Drops: None

Breeding: Meat (puppies from tamed dogs will be born tame)

Wolves spawn primarily in the taiga (snowy forest) and occasionally in forests, usually in packs. They attack sheep and rabbits, but will remain neutral unless they are hit, in which case they become hostile mobs and will fiercely attack, eyes glowing red.

You can tame a wolf, creating a dog, by feeding it bones until its hearts appear and a collar appears around its neck (collars are red, but can be dyed by right-clicking with dye in your hand).

Dogs are similar to cats, in that they will follow you unless you make them sit by right-clicking them. They will protect you from monsters, and are handy to travel with, though they do get too close to lava and fire sometimes. Still, they make good companions, at home and while adventuring.

Endermen

Drops: Ender pearls

Endermen are mobs that come from the End, but they can also spawn in the Overworld. They are not hostile unless you look them directly in the face, at which point they will attack. They teleport away from you and then back, making fighting a challenge. They are powerful and fierce and can teleport behind you when attacking, so be careful.

Unlike most hostile mobs, endermen aren't harmed by sunlight, but water (like rain) damages them. You can wear a pumpkin on your head and be safe to look at them, but your vision will be restricted if you do.

Ender pearls, dropped by endermen, are needed to craft Eyes of Ender to complete the End portal (you can also use an Eye of Ender to find the stronghold by throwing it in the air and following it). Otherwise, they can be used for swift transport, as you'll be teleported to the spot the ender pearl lands when thrown.

Although endermen are peaceful (unless you look at them), they can be frustrating because they like to pick up and move blocks, even ones that are part of your build.

Zombie pigmen

Drops: Rotten flesh, golden ingots, golden bars, and golden swords

Zombie pigmen spawn in the Nether, though they can cross through nether portals, and they are created when lightning strikes a pig, though this is rare.

Zombie pigmen are peaceful unless they are hit, but even one accidental bump will set them to attack—and they will call in their friends. They are ferocious fighters and will continue to fight you even if you die and respawn. They are happy to arm themselves in your gear as well, adding insult to injury. There are also baby zombie pigmen, which are faster and fiercer than their grown-up counterparts.

Hostile Mobs

Hostile mobs, or monsters, are the ones that you need to watch for (unless you play with your game set to peaceful, when they are harmless). Hostile mobs spawn only at night or in low light, and most catch fire when the sun comes up. Their drops can be useful—skeleton bones can be turned into bonemeal, used to help plants grow, and zombies and skeletons both drop armor and weapons.

Zombies, baby zombies, and zombie villagers

Drops: Raw flesh, and occasionally carrots, potatoes, iron bars, a piece of armor, shovels, or swords

Zombies spawn at night or in dark places. During the day, they will catch fire if they are in the sun, but they might be lurking in shady areas, such as under trees. If they attack you while on fire, you'll end up burning too, so be careful.

They are generally slow-moving (except for their babies) and are fairly easy to defeat if you are prepared. But if you don't have a good weapon or armor, they can still kill you. And even if you manage to kill one, it will summon other zombies to spawn in the area.

Zombies often wear armor, sometimes armor with minor enchantments, and some may carry a shovel or sword, making them a little harder to fight. On the bright side, they may also drop some of their weapons or gear when they die.

Baby zombies are a smaller, scarier version. They can fit into one-block openings, are super speedy, and can appear in daylight.

Zombie villagers are villagers that a zombie has attacked, so they still look like villagers—green, zombified ones. They can be turned back into villagers once you are able to make potions, but it is quite a process.

Skeletons

Drops: Bones, arrows, a bow, and armor

Skeletons in many ways are very similar to zombies; they spawn in the dark and burn in daylight, and are often wearing armor. Unlike zombies, they are able to attack from a distance with a bow and arrow, and they can shoot fast, knocking you back. For this reason, it is helpful to use a bow yourself.

Spiders, cave spiders, and spider jockeys

Drops: String and spider eyes

Spiders come in several varieties. The most common are large. Very occasionally they are ridden by skeleton jockeys, making them more dangerous at a distance. Spiders are faster than other mobs and can climb and jump, and they can fit through openings one block high and two blocks wide.

Cave spiders are even smaller and fit through small spaces. Even worse, they're venomous and their bite will make you sick (drinking milk from a pail will help heal you). They're found only in dungeons and abandoned mineshafts, where they come from spawners (surrounded by cobwebs), but they are vicious foes (a bucket of lava is a good weapon for destroying their nest and spawner).

Creepers

Drops: Gunpowder; if killed by a skeleton, a music disc

Creepers, the hissing, walking bushes that explode, have become one of the symbols of the game, as well as a source of frustration to anyone who has ever built on a survival map. Creepers attack by moving in close, hissing, and then exploding, destroying many blocks in the area when they do.

It is especially frustrating to have part of your house, your redstone wiring, or some other important work destroyed, so it is important to keep the area well lit. A few cats can help keep them away. It is possible, if you're alert, to catch them before they explode and at the very least lead them away, if not slay them outright.

Slimes

Drops: Slime balls

Bouncing green blocks that come in a variety of sizes, slimes spawn in swamps at night and sometimes in deep caves. They aren't hard to fight, because they move slowly, but once you hit one it will divide into two slimes, and those two will each divide, and so on until you find yourself surrounded by small slimes, which can't hurt you and are easy enough to defeat.

Each small slime drops a slime ball. Slime balls are needed to craft sticky pistons, leads, and fire charges.

Silverfish

Drops: None

Silverfish are small critters that hide in strongholds and the Extreme Hills biome. They are in blocks that look just like regular blocks—until you break them and silverfish appear. If you attack a silverfish, it will call others. They can start to do some damage as their numbers increase, to both you and the area. They will break blocks too (potentially releasing even more silverfish). They can't climb, so standing on a block and pouring lava is a quick way to deal with them.

Endermites

Drops: None

A newly introduced mob with the 1.8 update, endermites occasionally spawn instead of an enderman or when you throw an ender pearl. They are small purple bugs that emit particles, attack, and do more damage than silverfish, but they are easily defeated.

Witches

Drops: Bottles, glowstone dust, redstone, gunpowder, spider eyes, sugar, and sticks (except for sticks, all are potion ingredients)

Witches look like villagers garbed in witch gear. They can spawn anywhere at night and don't burn in the sun. They are quiet, can sneak up on you, and attack by throwing potions from a distance. They are also able to use potions to help themselves; if they are on fire or in lava they will drink a fire resist potion, for instance, and they are quick to heal themselves. Your best bet is to get some distance and use a bow and arrow, or just stay clear.

Guardian

Drops: Fish, prismarine crystal, prismarine shard

Guardians are a new mob, introduced with the 1.8 update. The first hostile ocean mob in the game, they are swift and fierce hunters usually found in and around ocean monuments. They can attack with spikes that they can extend and pull in (though the damage is minimal), but they also use a far more powerful beam of light to attack from a distance. They need to "charge" this beam before they can fire and will take a short period of time to recover before they can shoot again. They are formidable foes.

Guardians don't die when they are on land, but they will flop around and head for the closest body of water. If they are in shallow water, you can use a fishing rod to pull them to land and attack them there, which is far easier than fighting them in water.

Nether Mobs

Some mobs spawn only in the Nether. These mobs drop items that you can't get in the Overworld, such as wither skulls (needed to summon a wither) and blaze rods (used as fuel and needed in some recipes).

Wither skeletons

Drops: Bones, coal, stone swords, and wither skulls

Wither skeletons are found in nether fortresses and are more challenging to fight than their Overworld cousins, as they can cause the *wither effect*, which weakens you considerably for 10 seconds after being hit.

Every so often, a wither skeleton will drop its skull, which you will need in order to call the wither (see the "Bosses" section).

Wither skeletons often spawn near blaze spawners, leaving you open to a double attack. If you have a bow, you can fight from a distance, possibly from the shelter of the fortress, but you may knock them into the lava below the fortress, which means you won't be able to collect drops. They are best not faced up close unless you have good gear.

Blaze

Drops: Blaze rods (an alternative fuel for furnaces and an ingredient in potions)

Blaze are spinning, flying mobs that hover near their spawner in nether fortresses. They are creatures made of and armed with fire, and can be a challenge because they shoot fire at you from a distance. They are vulnerable to water, which can't be used in the Nether—unless you bring it in snowball form. Snowballs make a good distance weapon, though you're best off ensuring you also have fire resist enchants on your armor, or a heat-protecting potion on hand.

Ghasts

Drops: Ghast tears and gunpowder

A large, floating, tentacled mob that will shoot fireballs at you. Because they float out of sword range, a bow is your best weapon, though you can lure them to the ground to attack with a sword too. Just be careful on the uneven, lava-covered terrain to not fall to your death or trip into a pool of lava while dodging fireballs! Ghast tears are a rare potion ingredient, making fighting ghasts worthwhile.

Magma cubes

Drops: Magma cream

Magma cubes are very similar to slimes from the Overworld. They stretch like springs when they bounce and drop magma cream, needed for heat-resist potions. They will divide into smaller cubes as they are attacked, and the smallest have the possibility of dropping magma cream.

Player-Created Mobs

There are a couple of mobs that you can create as well; they can be used for defense and company.

Snow golems

Drops: Snowballs

Snow golems look like pumpkin-headed snowmen, and they leave a trail of snow when they move. They are easily crafted by stacking two blocks of snow and then putting a pumpkin on top (not on a crafting bench; you need to build the snowman). While they will throw snowballs at hostile mobs, this won't do much to slow them down; they're more useful for harvesting snow and snowballs or to create a snowy landscape.

Iron golems

Drops: Iron ingots and roses

Also craftable, iron golems are far more powerful than snow golems. While they occasionally spawn around NPC villages, you can also make them. Iron golems are not made on a crafting bench but rather built with four blocks of iron (two stacked and one on each side of the upper block, like a "T") and a pumpkin head.

Iron golems protect villagers before players, and won't leave the area if there are villagers to defend. They have a fierce attack, swinging their long arms and flinging enemies away. If you damage a villager, even if you created the golem, it will turn on you as well. Iron golems will sometimes offer a rose to a villager.

Bosses

Three larger, more powerful mobs, known as *bosses*, exist: Elder Guardians are considered mini-bosses, harder to fight than regular mobs; Withers can be summoned after collecting three wither skeleton heads and are a tougher foe than Elder Guardians; and the final, ultimate boss is the Ender Dragon, which spawns in the End.

Elder Guardian

Drops: Fish, prismarine crystal, prismarine shard, wet sponge

New to the game and considered a mini-boss, Elder Guardians are a larger, more dangerous version of guardians and are found inside ocean monuments.

They give a mining fatigue effect to all players within 50 blocks, which will slow you down considerably if you are trying to mine for treasure within the ocean monument. Like guardians, they use a beam to attack, as well as having spikes, but they are far more powerful and will even attack players in boats. They are incredibly hard to fight, and you will need your best gear, as well as water potions or enchants on your armor. Again, as with guardians, it is possible to draw them to dry land with a fishing rod, where you can attack more easily, but they will immediately try to get back into the water.

Withers

Drops: Nether star

A Wither is a strong boss that must be summoned using a soul sand cross and three wither skeleton skulls. You need to place the sand and skulls in a specific pattern and order (the last block placed must be a skull) for a Wither to appear.

A three-headed flying creature, the Wither shoots exploding skulls from all three of its heads. It also blasts the wither effect, which weakens all players hit by it. Some of the skulls will also damage nearby blocks (reducing places you might find to hide), and if a player is directly hit by a skull, the Wither will regain some health points.

Fighting a Wither is a big challenge, one best done with several players if you are on a multiplayer server. If you're on your own, try to summon it in a con- tained space with places to hide, have plenty of good gear and health potions, and take your time.

The Wither drops a Nether star, which is needed to light a beacon, a special beam of light that extends to the sky and provides a special effect (such as haste, which makes you mine faster) to all the players in an area.

Ender dragon

Drops: Dragon egg

The Ender Dragon is the ultimate boss in Minecraft. Only found in the End, which is also populated by endermen, the Ender Dragon is a huge monster that flies in to attack players and can do damage with its head, wings, and body.

The Ender Dragon has a health bar so that you can track the damage you do. You'll also note that it regains health from the crystals on obsidian towers scattered about the End. It's a good plan to destroy the crystals so that the dragon can't heal as you're fighting it. The dragon can also explode blocks as it passes, so be careful of falling debris when you fight. You can use a bow and arrow or wait for it to swoop low (this is more risky). Its head is the most vulnerable place for players to strike.

When you defeat the Ender Dragon, you will get a dragon egg and lots of experience points, and the game credits will roll. This is, of course, not the end of the game, as there is no end point in Minecraft, so you'll be able to return to your world and continue your adventures wealthier and with more experience.

Unlimited Possibilities

This has just been the barest peek at some of what Minecraft has to offer. Hopefully you have a good taste of some of the possibilities that await you. What we can't discuss here is what you yourself bring to the game—creativity, fresh ideas, innovative designs, and ground-breaking strategies. Whether you play on your own or with others, whether you like to explore and discover or would rather look things up and learn from others, the game you play will be unique to you, something of your own creation.

Minecraft is the perfect opportunity to take risks, experiment, try new things, and see what you can do. You can share your creations and work with others, or keep it just for yourself. The opportunities are unlimited—have fun exploring them!

PART 3

MORE THAN JUST BUILDING—CREATING

There's much more to Minecraft than mining and crafting. Minecraft is a sandbox game, which means you'll set your own goals and invent your own methods to achieve them. You might have a goal to live as a nomad, exploring and never staying in one place for too long, or you might decide to build a city, or you might set out to explore every feature Minecraft has to offer.

No matter your goal, you'll need to build some sort of structure along the way. As a nomad, you might encounter places you'd previously explored. It's fun to see your finished structures dotting the landscape, hinting at a previous civilization. If you choose to build a city, you'll be working on multiple structures, and you'll need a lot of materials and easy, efficient methods of gathering. While exploring every feature of the game, you'll need to make sure your basics are taken care of: safety, food, and storage.

And above all, you'll incorporate style and your own personal flair. This book will show you how to stay safe while building and how to mass-produce materials, and it will give you tips for making your structures look and feel interesting and complete.

There's No Place Like Home

Once you've settled on a world, gathered some food, and found a nice place to call home, it's time to think about building. Housing is the logical first step. A decent house will provide safety from the mobs, a secure place to respawn upon death, and with a little bit of effort, something that looks great. On multiplayer servers, a well-designed home is a good way to leave a unique mark.

More often than not, your first home will be a hole in the side of a hill, a hole in the ground, or a structure that is a patchwork of whatever blocks you happen to have in your inventory (usually dirt or cobblestone). But if you put some time into it, you can turn that hasty survival shelter into a real architectural achievement.

Safety First!

No matter how meager or extravagant your home, it's important to be diligent in protecting it. That means preventing aggressive mobs from spawning near your house and ensuring that they can't wander in uninvited. Fire is another hazard, which we'll address when we begin adding fireplaces and other aesthetics.

Lighting

In Minecraft, light comes from various sources, such as the sun, moon, torches, fire, and other light-emitting blocks. Each light source has an intensity associated with it that is measured in levels. Aggressive mobs (creepers, endermen, skeletons, and zombies) spawn at lighting levels below 8. A block fully exposed to sunlight has a light level of 15, while moonlight has a level of 4.

The light level of blocks that emit light is highest at their source and decreases by 1 in each of the cardinal directions (north, south, east, and west) and vertically (**Figure 5.1**). It decreases by 2 diagonally.

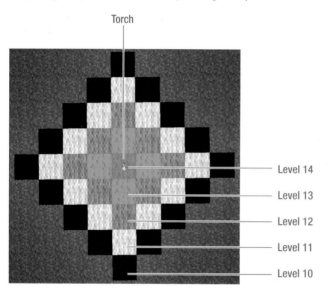

Torch

Level 14

Level 13

Level 12

Level 11

Level 10

FIGURE 5.1 Lighting levels from a single torch without another source overlapping.

For example, torches have a light level of 14, so the block the torch is placed on has a light level of 14. Moving north, and assuming there are no obstructions, the block immediately adjacent has a level of 13, the next a level of 12, and so on. The block immediately diagonally adjacent has a light level of 12, the next a level of 10, and so on.

Be sure to fully illuminate the inside of your house, an area around it, and the paths leading to it. And it's important, but often overlooked, to light up the roof. It would be unfortunate to have a creeper drop off the roof on top of you during a mad dash back to your house.

Access to Your House

Although lighting will prevent hostile mobs from spawning, it won't prevent them from following you into the lighted area. Ensuring that your house is and remains fully enclosed is paramount. In the unfortunate event a creeper manages to explode near your house, it's important to patch the hole as soon as possible.

Building a fence around the outer edge of your lit area is another useful technique, because mobs can't climb fences. Cover or fence off any cave entrance until you're ready to explore it.

Fire

Many blocks are flammable. For example, wood, planks, wool, leaves, and vines can all catch fire. Fire can spread from a burning block 1 block in any direction horizontally, 1 block below, and up to 4 blocks above it. Flint and steel will immediately start a fire when used.

Although lava may seem like a good lighting source in your house, it's most often not. In **Figure 5.2**, I've attempted to use lava behind glass as ambient lighting. But in this case, the wood is too close to the lava, so it has caught on fire and the fire has spread to the floor. Still (non-flowing) lava can ignite flammable blocks. In the next chapter, we'll explore how to use lava safely inside a flammable structure.

Lightning strikes produce fire at the site of the strike. Most often, rain will immediately extinguish the flame before it spreads, but if you see fire on or near flammable blocks on your structure, it's not a bad idea to manually extinguish it by left-clicking the side of the block that's on fire or by pouring a bucket of water on the flame.

FIGURE 5.2 Still lava does not work as a lighting source here, because it is too close to flammable building material.

Your First Shelter

Once you are ready to build your first shelter, there are a few decisions to make. Some will depend on what type of shelter you choose, and others will apply to all shelters. Ideally, your chosen site will border a body of water (pond, lake, river), because that will allow you to start growing crops without having to craft a bucket to move water.

Building vs. Carving

You have two ways to create a shelter: building from scratch and carving into the landscape.

Building out in the open is more time consuming. First you must gather the building materials required, construct the shelter, and finally light up a larger area around it. Adding onto the shelter at night is an extra challenge. And of course, the initial material cost is much greater when building from scratch.

When carving, after you've lit up your living space, you can add lighting as you expand into the landscape. Mobs can't move through blocks, so unless you've left a hole from the outside into your room—or you fall into a cavern—you shouldn't encounter any hostile mobs as you work. This method is quick and particularly useful if you've been unable to place a bed before needing to shelter. Beds allow you to set a spawn point and sleep, which skips the night and turns it day, so you should craft, place, and sleep in one as soon as possible.

Even if you prefer to live above ground or out in the open, carving a room into the landscape is a fast, easy way to maintain relative safety at night.

Necessary Items

Whether you choose to build your first shelter or carve it in the side of a hill, it should have a few essentials placed fairly compactly. A bed, a crafting table, at least one chest, and a furnace are the minimum requirements. Later, when you expand, you'll likely no longer be bound by space constraints, but your bedroom should include these same items and your chest should include some emergency items, such as a spare set of armor, a spare set of tools, and a stash of food.

A bed can be placed against a wall, but there should be 2 blocks of open air above it and 1 block of open air along at least one side to ensure that you don't spawn outside your shelter when you awaken or respawn from death.

A chest can't open if there's a block (such as a crafting table) above it, but it can if there's another chest. You can use this feature to build relatively compact storage facilities. You can place crafting tables and furnaces on top of or next to each other. Hold the Shift key while right-clicking the top face of a crafting table or furnace to place something on top of it.

Examples

The shelter in **Figure 5.3** is about as compact as you can make it while still being able to call it a structure. For this structure you'll need several blocks: 12 wood, 8 cobblestone, and 3 wool. You'll place 11 wood blocks in a crafting grid to convert them to 44 wood planks. One of those planks will be used to smelt the last piece of wood in the furnace in order to obtain the charcoal needed for the torch. If you happen to have a piece of coal, you can omit the extra step of producing charcoal, which brings the wood count to 11. The shell of the shelter will comprise 26 wood planks. It's not necessary to place blocks on the outside corners of this shelter.

FIGURE 5.3 Here is an example of the most compact shelter you can build. As you can see, I've managed to include the essentials—bed, chest, crafting table, furnace, and torch—in an area that is 2 blocks deep by 3 blocks wide by 2 blocks high.

When you're ready to sleep the night away or in need of quick protection, place 6 wood planks on top of the space marked with orange wool. This will prevent mobs from getting near you to attack.

In **Figure 5.4**, the shelter is carved into the side of a mountain. You'll need 5 wood blocks (6 if you're making charcoal), 8 cobblestone, and 3 wool. Here, you'll use the cobblestone gathered from carving out the shelter rather than finding another source.

FIGURE 5.4 I've used glass to allow you to see into this shelter, but you could build this shelter without carving out those 4 blocks.

When you're ready to sleep the night away or in need of quick protection, 2 cobblestone blocks, taken from what you carved, can be placed on top of the orange wool to keep the mobs out of your shelter.

Style

The creative freedom that Minecraft's open world, landscape, and material diversity allow is one of the myriad reasons the game is as popular as it is. Many players challenge themselves to imitate real-life structures and styles— castles and modern skyscrapers, for example. Some players go in a completely different and unique direction. Because the blocks are 1 meter by 1 meter, you have to get creative when duplicating real-world architecture, but with a little bit of ingenuity you can get pretty close.

Cape Cod

The Cape Cod style originated in New England in the 17th century. New England winters, especially on the coast, are cold, windy, and snow-filled. The steeply sloped roof ensures that snow doesn't pile up. The house's symmetrical design and small size make it easy to build, with a relatively low material cost. Its central chimney, fireplaces in each room, and low ceilings make it easy to heat (**Figure 5.5**).

FIGURE 5.5 This house is based on the Cape Code style. I've used cobblestone for the base, oak wooden planks for the siding, and spruce stairs for the roof.

Two basic shapes make up the Cape Cod style: a cuboid for the living area and a triangle for the roof. In this build, you use stairs to give the roof its sloped look. The most expensive piece of this build is the chimney, because it is made of brick. You'll need to spend extra time exploring for clay, which needs to be processed in a furnace before you can craft it into the brick block.

Modern

The modern style is good to move on to once you've mastered basic structures. Modern builds can look interesting with very little effort. Characteristics of modern structures include simple, strong lines with 90-degree angles. Materials are often simple and duplicated throughout the structure. Glass is heavily used. The blocky style is easily replicated in the Minecraft world.

There are many variations of the modern style, but a good place to start is to draw inspiration from the architect Frank Lloyd Wright, one of the founders of the modern movement (**Figure 5.6**). Wright called his philosophy organic and sought to maintain harmony between nature and architecture. His masterpiece Fallingwater seamlessly integrates the waterfall it sits upon into the structure of the house. The landscape of Minecraft is well suited to such structures, especially where there are cliffs, as in the extreme hills biome.

FIGURE 5.6 This house is loosely based on one of Frank Lloyd Wright's most famous buildings, Fallingwater. You can learn more about it at www.fallingwater.org.

Summary

Seeing your creativity evolve as you move from building your first shelter to some of the more complex structures and balancing aesthetics with practicality (and, of course, safety) is rewarding. You're not limited to living in a box made of cobblestone, nor are you limited to imitating real-life styles and structures. By mixing materials and styles, and adding your personal touch, you'll create something truly unique.

Not Finished Until It's Furnished

Once you've completed the outside of your structure, you might think "OK, now what do I put inside?" or "How do I decorate this?" Minecraft has crafting recipes for household items that can add some style (paintings, flower pots, stained glass), but it lacks some of the basics, such as furniture. Sure, you can make a bed, and although it's useful for resetting your spawn point and skipping the nighttime, it's not very appealing. In short, it's ugly. It's not impossible to furnish a house; you just have to get creative and use items in a way they weren't necessarily intended to be used—wooden pressure plates as tabletops, for example.

As with the outside of your building, personal taste will ultimately dictate what you add to the interior, but pushing yourself to try a new method or add a new element can be very rewarding.

Lighting

Lighting is essential to prevent the spawning of hostile mobs, and it can also be used as a design element. Experiment with different fixtures and light sources to see how they change the style and mood of your dwelling. The materials you choose when building your structure will alter your perception of brightness and have an effect on the feel of room. For instance, if your primary building material is quartz, which is white, your room will seem brighter than if you had used black stained clay. If you go too dark, instead of the open feel you were hoping for, your building might feel cramped and claustrophobic. Go too bright, and instead of feeling like a cozy home, it might feel like a supermarket or doctor's office.

Light Sources

There are a handful of light-emitting blocks that are specifically designed for lighting: torches, jack-o'-lanterns, glowstone blocks, and redstone lamps (**Figure 6.1**).

FIGURE 6.1 Left to right: Torch, jack-o'-lantern, glowstone block, illuminated redstone lamp.

Glowstone blocks function underwater. Redstone lamps can as well, but you must take care to protect the circuit. Water washes away redstone, buttons, and levers. Jack-o'-lanterns can be placed underwater, but submerged or not, they need to be placed on top of another block.

There are three other light sources you can use: fire, lava, and beacons. But these have caveats: Fire and lava ignite flammable blocks, and beacons are too expensive to be anything more than a novelty (**Figure 6.2**). Beacons, like glowstone and redstone lamps, function underwater.

FIGURE 6.2 Left to right: Fire burning indefinitely on netherrack, lava enclosed in glass, and a beacon.

Water extinguishes fire, of course, and fire burns indefinitely only on netherrack. Lava doesn't work underwater, because it interacts with water to create obsidian, stone, or cobblestone.

Sea lanterns have been added in Minecraft version 1.8 (**Figure 6.3**). They're found in ocean monuments and their properties are similar to glowstone.

FIGURE 6.3 Sea lanterns.

Let's take a closer look at the sources available now and the light levels they produce.

- Torches have a light level of 14. They are cheap and easy to craft. Just one piece of coal or charcoal and a stick produces 4 torches, and since trees are a renewable resource, you have unlimited resources for torches.
- Jack-o'-lanterns have a light level of 15. As with torches, they are relatively inexpensive. They're crafted with a torch and pumpkin. Once crafted, they have a face on one side.

- Glowstone blocks have a light level of 15. You can mine them in the nether.

- Redstone lamps have a light level of 15. They have a look reminiscent of a Victorian lantern. Redstone lamps must receive a redstone signal in order to emit light. You can use a simple mechanism such as an activated lever or a redstone torch placed directly on or next to the block. You can wire multiple lamps to a single lever, allowing you to walk into a room and "turn on the lights." Or, you can wire them to a daylight sensor, allowing you to have lamps that automatically turn on as the sun sets.

- Beacons give off light but are very expensive. Their benefit is in the ability to provide you powers, similar to some potions, if you're in range. Among the powers are speed, which increases your movement speed, and haste, which gives a boost to how quickly you can mine blocks. It's useful to include at least one beacon in your build.

- Lava has a light level of 15, and you can use it in a number of creative ways. For example, try surrounding lava with glass to make a sort of tube, and letting it flow to enhance a futuristic or laboratory theme.

- Fire has a light level of 15. There's very little practicality to using fire (by igniting netherrack) as a primary light source. But it can look really cool on a monumental pillar (**Figure 6.4**).

FIGURE 6.4 Ignite netherrack on top of a monumental pillar for a classical feel.

Sconces

Sconces are light fixtures that are attached directly to the wall. A torch, when placed on a wall, is a sconce. While it does the job of lighting an area, you can add some style to it.

Item frames allow you to display a smaller version of a block. Generally, if you place an item that emits light in an item frame, it will not emit light. However, a neat trick in item placement allows you to get around this limitation and imitate a sconce—just place the item frame on the block after a torch has been placed (**Figure 6.5**).

FIGURE 6.5 Starting from the far right, we have a torch placed on a wall, an item frame placed behind a torch, and an item frame with a mossy cobblestone wall placed in it and rotated.

To create your sconce, place your torch on a block, then aim your reticle (the crosshairs in the middle of your screen) at the face of the block on which the torch is placed (not at the torch itself) and right-click to place the item frame.

This is an improvement over a naked torch, but you can take it a step further and place an item into the item frame to give the sconce some texture. While any item can be used, there are a few that work particularly well. Cobblestone walls, mossy cobblestone walls, and half slabs give the appearance that the torch is being held in place. Fences and gates give the appearance that the torch is clipped onto the frame.

To add an item to the item frame, aim your reticle at the item frame (again, not at the torch) and right-click with the chosen item in your hand. Right-click the item frame again to rotate the item in the frame.

Recessed Lighting

Recessed lighting is set into walls, ceilings, or floors. This type of lighting isn't as efficient at stopping mobs from spawning because the light source sits farther away from the ground, but it can make the lighting really feel like a part of the structure rather than an add-on to the interior.

In recessed lighting on the ceiling and walls, you don't have to place a glass block in front of the torch, but it does make the fixture feel more finished (**Figure 6.6**). However, because torches aren't a block and you can't stand on them, if you use recessed lighting in the floor, you will need something to cover them so you don't find yourself falling into the recesses.

FIGURE 6.6 The example on the left is a recess without a glass block or pane in front of it. The torch on the right is set farther back and has a glass block placed in front of it.

Chandeliers

Chandeliers are light fixtures hung from a ceiling. In Minecraft you can achieve this same effect by using wooden or nether brick fences to imitate the framework. Torches cannot be placed on the sides of fences but can be placed on top (**Figure 6.7**).

FIGURE 6.7 Here, two fence posts are placed end to end from the ceiling, with a fence attached to each side of the lowest fence post.

You can use glass panes to add complexity and a little glimmer to the chandelier. They can be as simple as in **Figure 6.8** or built to look endlessly complex, as in **Figure 6.9**. Of course, the larger the chandelier, the more space required. It's easy to get caught in the trap of building a small room and then deciding to add a chandelier only to end up with a room completely dominated by the light fixture.

FIGURE 6.8 Two fence posts are placed end to end from the ceiling. A glowstone block is placed on the bottom face of the lower fence post. Eight glass panes are placed around the glowstone block.

FIGURE 6.9 I've added 16 glass panes to the set of 8 already placed. I've also added a layer of 8 panes to the bottom.

You can use glowstone blocks and redstone lamps to create a sort of flower, which can be built however you see fit. Remember that redstone lamps need a signal to function. Most people prefer to hide the circuitry, as in **Figure 6.10**.

FIGURE 6.10 Two fence posts extend end to end from the ceiling. Hidden behind the lamps is a redstone torch or activated lever placed on top of the block of quartz. The end of the fence post won't be fully enclosed, but since you'll be standing on the ground most of the time, you likely won't notice it.

If you choose to use lava, it should be enclosed in glass. Wooden fences are flammable, so you must use a nether brick fence if you want to suspend it from the ceiling.

Lampposts

Lampposts can add style to your walkways. In much the same way you used fences to suspend chandeliers from the ceiling, you can use them to elevate lights from the ground (**Figure 6.11**). In fact, you can take a couple of the chandelier examples (Figures 6.7–6.9) and just move the fences to the bottom. Lampposts typically shouldn't be too ostentatious, especially when they line a path. You don't want your path looking too cluttered.

FIGURE 6.11 Four lamppost styles, simple to complex. From left: A torch on fence posts, a wooden plank block placed on fence posts with torches on four sides, glowstone blocks atop nether brick fence posts, and a redstone lamp flower.

The Entrance

The entrance to your house sets the stage for your visitors. It can make your house look warm and inviting or cool and modern. At its most basic level, a good entrance will allow you to enter and exit your structure easily. But if you take a little time to try out some of the game's options, you can create a custom door that will complete the exterior of your structure.

Doors

Minecraft has wooden and iron doors. Both can be placed as single or double doors (**Figure 6.12**).

Wooden doors are easily broken with an axe. Zombies can break through wooden doors. To open a wooden door, simply aim your reticle at the door and right-click.

FIGURE 6.12 Single doors and double doors. Oak wooden on the left, iron on the right.

There are a number of ways to rig your door. You can use redstone torches, buttons, levers, and pressure plates to open and close them. These switches are optional for wooden doors, but you cannot open an iron door without them.

If you are using buttons and levers, you must place them on the floor in front of a door or on the wall next to or above a door (**Figure 6.13**). To "press" a button or "flip" a lever, aim your reticle at it and right-click. Buttons will open your door momentarily, and then close it. Levers will allow you to hold your door open or closed.

If you are using pressure plates and redstone torches, you will need to place them on the floor in front of a door (**Figure 6.14**). Redstone torches will open your door and keep it open. A pressure plate, activated by walking over it, will hold your door open as long as you're standing on the plate. Remember that if you put pressure plates on the outside of your doors, mobs can activate them too.

FIGURE 6.13 A lever placed in any of the positions shown here will interact with a door.

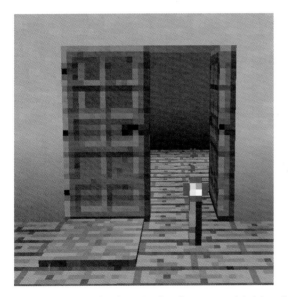

FIGURE 6.14 A redstone torch and a pressure plate interacting with a door. The pressure plate is inactive until a player or mob steps on it.

Pistons

Try using pistons and sticky pistons to create an automated entrance. Pistons, when activated by redstone, extend and push blocks. When deactivated, the piston retracts and the block is left where it was pushed. Sticky pistons, when activated, extend and push a block and will pull the block back into place when deactivated (**Figure 6.15**).

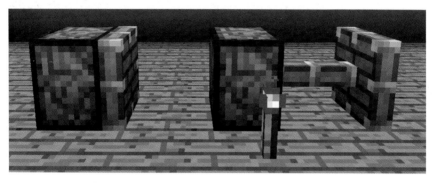

FIGURE 6.15 On the left is a piston in its default state. On the right is a piston extended by an activated redstone torch.

You can use pistons to create hidden entrances, rooms, and trapdoors. They may not grant any benefit over doors, but they look and sound awesome. To create the example in **Figure 6.16,** place two stacks of two sticky pistons 4 blocks apart. Then place a block of any material (white stained clay in this example) in front of each of the sticky pistons. Next, place a block directly behind each of the lower pistons. Placing a redstone torch on top of the block will cause the pistons to extend, which closes the entrance. Removing the redstone torch will cause the pistons to retract and open the entrance.

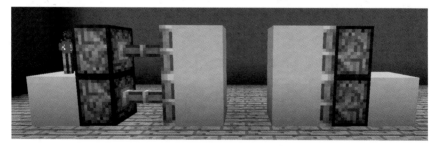

FIGURE 6.16 An entrance constructed with pistons. A redstone torch activates the stack on the left. If you were to activate the stack on the right, the entrance would be closed.

Flooring

Lots of block types in Minecraft can be suitable for flooring, but raw resources such as wood and stone can leave your structure feeling incomplete. Instead of wood, try using wooden planks (crafted from wood). Each of the types of trees in Minecraft gives you a different colored plank block (**Figure 6.17**).

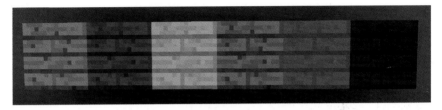

FIGURE 6.17 Each of the different types of wooden plank blocks. From left to right: oak, spruce, birch, jungle, acacia, and dark oak.

Instead of stone, you might try stone bricks. Instead of clay, try hardened clay. Or take it a step further and try dyeing your hardened clay.

By combining different colors or types of blocks, you can put together some interesting patterns (**Figure 6.18**).

FIGURE 6.18 Black stained clay alternated with quartz blocks gives you a checkerboard floor, like you might see in a kitchen.

You can also add detail to your floor by changing the blocks on the edge to a different but complementary material (**Figure 6.19**). This can be a great way to transition from one type of material to another.

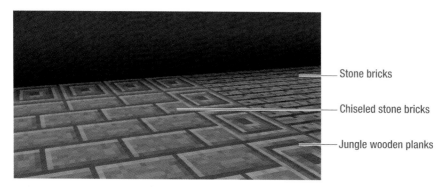

Stone bricks

Chiseled stone bricks

Jungle wooden planks

FIGURE 6.19 Here, the primary material used for the floor is stone brick. It's edged with chiseled stone bricks. Chiseled stone also separates the stone brick from the jungle wooden planks.

As an alternative to blocks for the floor, you can use carpet. Carpet placed on a block gives the block a different texture and color. This is especially handy because the blocks you use for your ceiling will become the floor of the room above. Carpet is crafted from wool. You can craft colored carpet from colored wool. There are 16 colors, including white. You could place a single color of carpet, create a pattern with two or more colors, or just add an accent (**Figure 6.20**).

FIGURE 6.20 Here, you're looking from the top down. On the left, blue carpet is alternated with light-blue carpet. On the right, the red accent stands out against the field of white.

Furniture

No structure will look complete without some sort of furniture. As mentioned, aside from a bed, Minecraft doesn't have crafting recipes for furniture. But you can combine different blocks to imitate it. The furniture you build will not be functional, but it will bring your structure one step closer to looking and feeling complete.

Beds

The craftable bed looks out of place in any room much larger than the shelter you spent your first night in.

You can construct a more stylish bed, but you won't be able to sleep in it. Place 4 red wool blocks on the ground in a square. On the side you'd like the "pillows," place 2 white wool blocks side by side. Finally, place 1 light gray carpet on each of the white wool blocks (**Figure 6.21**). You can, of course, use any color combination you'd like.

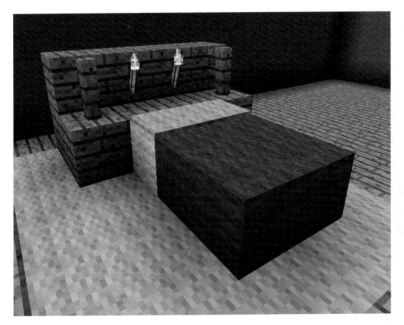

FIGURE 6.21 A stylish but less functional bed.

Chairs, Sofas, and Benches

Chairs are fairly easy to construct. Simply place a stair block and attach a sign to each side of the stairs (**Figure 6.22**). Place two stairs next to each other and signs on the end to make a sofa.

FIGURE 6.22 On the left is a simple armchair. On the right is a sofa.

You can use benches to add detail to your halls, paths, and sitting rooms. Benches have the same basic construction as chairs and sofas, but instead of stairs, you'll use slabs (**Figure 6.23**).

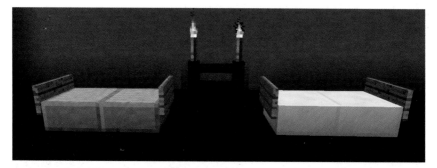

FIGURE 6.23 A bench constructed from slabs (stone on the left and quartz on the right).

Tables

You can make a basic table by placing a fence post on the ground and placing a pressure plate or a carpet block on top of it (**Figure 6.24**). If you're building a larger table, use carpet for the top. Pressure plates don't connect to each other, but carpet does.

FIGURE 6.24 A basic table made with a fence post and a pressure plate.

Use cobblestone walls as the base instead of a fence to give some heft to your table (**Figure 6.25**).

FIGURE 6.25 A table constructed from cobblestone walls and brown carpet, with an armchair at the end.

Appliances

Why stop at furniture? Why don't you go the extra mile and construct appliances?

You can construct a refrigerator by placing 2 iron blocks, one on top of the other, and then placing an iron door on one of the faces. Finally, place a lever on the left or right side of one of the iron blocks (**Figure 6.26**). When the lever is activated, the door will open.

FIGURE 6.26 A refrigerator.

It can be tricky to get the door positioned just right. With the iron door in hand, stand immediately to the left or right of the iron blocks, aim your reticle at the block on the floor in front of the iron blocks (you should be aiming diagonally downward) (**Figure 6.27**), and right-click to place your door. If you did it correctly, the door should sit right up against the iron blocks.

You can take this a step further and create an appliance that will dispense food or other items for you. Dispensers spit items out of their front face. They can also spit items through blocks. You could just stick a button on the dispenser, but since aesthetics are key, you're going to want to make it look better.

FIGURE 6.27 On the left side of the image, 2 iron blocks are stacked. The reticle is aimed at the-black stained clay immediately in front of the iron blocks.

For this version of the refrigerator, craft a dispenser and place it on top of a block set into the wall. Right-click the dispenser to open the interface, and place some food in the inventory slot. Place 2 iron blocks, one on top of the other, on the floor in front of the dispenser. Finally, place a button on the iron block in front of the dispenser (**Figure 6.28**). When activated, the button will send a signal to the dispenser and the dispenser will shoot one item from any of its inventory slots through the block in front of it.

FIGURE 6.28 From left to right, the steps required to construct a dispenser that looks like a refrigerator.

It doesn't take much to fashion a stove. Place a weighted (heavy) or stone pressure plate on top of a furnace (**Figure 6.29**). To place a pressure plate on top of the furnace without opening the furnace's interface, hold the pressure plate in your hand, aim at the top face of the furnace, hold the Shift key, and right-click.

FIGURE 6.29 Two stoves. Weighted pressure plate on the left, stone on the right.

Wall Decorations

Very quickly you'll begin to feel that your walls are lacking charm. Fortunately, there are a 2 items in Minecraft—item frames and paintings—that can help.

Paintings

When crafted, paintings have a generic texture. However, when placed on a wall, the game will randomly choose one of the 26 included images to display on the wall. The images range in size from 1 block wide by 1 block tall to 4 blocks wide by 4 blocks tall (**Figure 6.30**). This range allows you to adorn the walls of both small and large rooms.

FIGURE 6.30 On the left is a 1x1 block painting; on the right is a 4x4 block painting. All the paintings available are re-creations of paintings by Swedish artist Kristoffer Zetterstrand. His work can be found at www.zetterstrand.com.

Item Frames

Item frames can be placed on a wall and can hold a single item of any type. Light-emitting blocks, when placed in an item frame, will not emit light. You might keep a spare set of tools (**Figure 6.31**) or armor in an item frame. To retrieve your item once it's in the frame, right-click the frame.

FIGURE 6.31 A set of iron tools placed in item frames.

Item frames can be helpful in storage rooms. For example, if you have a chest full of cobblestone, you can label the chest by placing an item frame on the wall next to the chest and placing a cobblestone block in the frame. Or, if you have a chest that holds a mix of different organic material (seeds, carrots, saplings, and more), one of those items in a frame could remind you of the type of items in that chest.

The best features of item frames are the ability to display a map of your world, a working clock to give you the in-game time of day, and a compass to always point to the world's spawn point (**Figure 6.32**).

FIGURE 6.32 From left to right: a map, clock, and compass placed in item frames.

Windows

Windows will let in natural light and help keep the mobs out while still allowing you to see outside. Windows can also help make a room feel more open.

Materials

You have a couple of ways to construct windows. You can use glass blocks or you can use panes, which are crafted from glass blocks. Panes are significantly cheaper than glass blocks—you get 16 panes from 6 glass blocks.

Glass blocks, when placed, sit flush with the edges of the blocks around them. Panes are thinner than glass blocks and sit in the middle of the space usually occupied by a full block (**Figure 6.33**).

FIGURE 6.33 A glass block is on the left, and a pane is on the right.

Additionally, you can craft stained glass from glass blocks and dye. And from the stained glass, you can craft stained-glass panes. There are 16 colors of dye, including white, that you can use to craft colored stained glass (**Figure 6.34**).

FIGURE 6.34 A light blue stained-glass block on the left and a light blue pane on the right.

Design Example

While rectangular windows are easy to add to a structure after it's built, a little planning can give ordinary windows a nice boost.

Vary your materials. Instead of using a single color, like the light gray stained glass in **Figure 6.35**, add a simple shape made from black stained glass to the middle of the window.

FIGURE 6.35 A not-so-ordinary window.

Organic Adornments

Add some organic material to your structure to help it come alive.

Flower Pots

Flower pots are crafted from three bricks. They can hold flowers (1 block high), including dandelions, poppies, and tulips, cacti, saplings, and mushrooms

(**Figure 6.36**). Hold the flower pot and right-click on top of a block to place it. Then hold a 1-block-high flower and right-click the flower pot. Flowers can be found growing on grass throughout your world. You can also right-click a patch of grass while holding bonemeal (crafted from bones) to grow flowers—along with tall grass.

FIGURE 6.36 Flower pots holding a red tulip on the left, a birch sapling in the middle, and a mushroom on the right.

Window Boxes

Window boxes are mini gardens attached to the wall just outside a window. To construct a window box, start by placing dirt blocks against the outside wall just under a window. Place signs on both ends of the row of dirt blocks and also along the front. This will make the dirt blocks look as if they are being held against your structure. Plant some flowers or saplings in the dirt blocks (**Figure 6.37**).

FIGURE 6.37 A window box.

More Organics

While flower pots can display some plant material, they can't hold all the plant types that Minecraft offers: sugar canes and vines, for example. A great way to bring these elements inside is to create an "organic installation."

Sugar canes and vines look great when paired with quartz blocks. Sugar cane needs to be planted on dirt or sand, and the dirt or sand needs to be adjacent to water. You can take advantage of this to add yet one more interesting design element to your installation. Vines can be placed on any block and will grow down and to the sides. Add a light source to complete the installation (**Figure 6.38**).

FIGURE 6.38 A completed organic installation. Quartz blocks make up the main structure. Glowstone blocks are placed in the ceiling of the installation, vines on the back wall. The front is left open except for the light-gray glass panes providing a barrier.

You don't have to limit yourself to flower pots, window boxes, or full organic installations to bring a little green inside. For example, try taking the window box idea and bringing it inside. Place a dirt block on the floor in a corner of a room. Place a sign on each of the sides not touching a wall, and then plant a sapling or other flower. A caveat to using saplings is that if there is enough room, the sapling will grow. So make sure there are 4 blocks or less of open space above the sapling for oak, 6 for birch, and 7 for the other varieties.

Summary

You don't have to settle for bland! You've spent a lot of time building your structure, so don't skimp on decorating. Whether you opt for the modern feel of minimalist design or prefer the natural ambiance of organic materials, spending some time on the interior will make your structure feel like home.

Supporting Your Lifestyle

As time passes in your world, you will reach a point when you need more of, well, everything, but especially food and wood. You need a farm for each of the different types of food, a mine for pulling materials out of the ground, and of course, you're going to need a place to store all your items.

Storage Room

Your personal inventory and your first few chests will likely be unorganized as you get settled in the world. But if you build a storage room or facility that is easy to expand, you'll be able to keep everything organized and reduce the amount of time you spend grabbing materials from your stores, giving you more time to build.

Chests

When you place a chest on the ground, it will be a single chest. Place another chest adjacent to it to turn it into a double chest (**Figure 7.1**). A double chest gives you twice the inventory of a single chest.

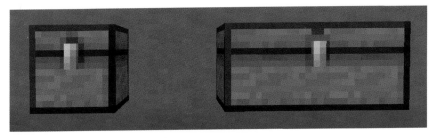

FIGURE 7.1 On the left is a single chest. On the right is a double chest.

Once you've created a double chest, you cannot place another chest adjacent to it. The area immediately above a chest must be free of obstruction for the chest to open. There is, however, an exception to this rule: Place another chest above or below it and it will still function (**Figure 7.2**).

FIGURE 7.2 Chests will still function with other chests on top of them.

While the amount of materials you're storing will ultimately dictate the size of your storage area, you can use this feature to construct a fairly compact storage room.

Labels

There are a couple of ways to label your chests. Signs, when placed on the ground or on a wall, allow you to write up to four lines of text. Each line has a maximum of 15 characters, including spaces and punctuation. You could, for example, place a sign on a column next to a chest and write what's in the chest. For more compact signage, place a sign on a column between two chests. On the first line, write what's in the chest to the left. On the second, "write" an arrow pointing to the chest on the left. On the third line, write what's in the chest on the right. On the fourth line, write an arrow pointing to the chest on the right (**Figure 7.3**).

FIGURE 7.3 Signs can be used to provide a textual guide to your storage room.

You can use item frames to give you a visual guide to your storage room (**Figure 7.4**). Place an item frame on the wall next to a chest, and place an item (representative of what's in the chest next to it) in the frame.

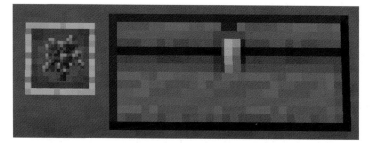

FIGURE 7.4 Using item frames isn't as compact as signs, but it can look nicer. The oak sapling in the item frame could be a signal to you that the chest contains oak saplings or other organic material.

Design Example

In **Figure 7.5**, the chests on the right use item frames as labels. The chests on the left use signs. The columns are made from spruce wood. Glowstone blocks are used for lighting to keep the room compact and uncluttered. Jungle wood planks are used as the primary material for the floor.

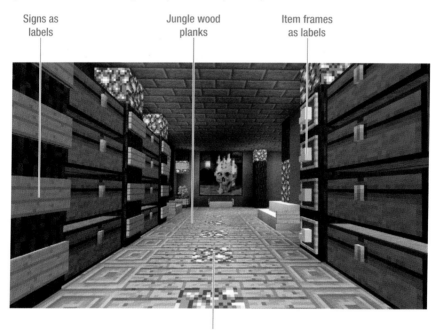

Signs as labels   Jungle wood planks   Item frames as labels

Glowstone

FIGURE 7.5 A completed storage room.

Farming

The goal of any farm is to mass produce materials easily and efficiently. An efficient farm will keep your supplies well stocked with little effort.

Plants for Food

Wheat is grown from seeds, carrots are grown from other carrots, and potatoes grow from other potatoes. You can acquire wheat seeds by breaking tall grass.

Carrots and potatoes can be found in world-generated villages. Rarely, they will drop when you kill a zombie.

In order to grow plants, each type of crop needs to be planted on dirt that has been tilled with a hoe (**Figure 7.6**) and is within 4 blocks of water. The water can be still or flowing.

FIGURE 7.6 From left to right: a dirt block, a tilled dirt block, and planted wheat.

When each crop is fully grown (**Figure 7.7**), aim at the crop and left-click to harvest the crop. Wheat will drop one wheat and up to three seeds. Carrots and potatoes will drop up to four of each. Be careful: Potatoes have a chance of dropping a poisonous potato.

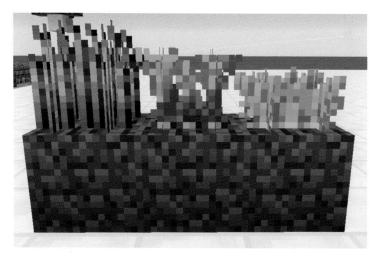

FIGURE 7.7 From left to right: fully grown wheat, carrots, and potatoes.

Plant Farm

Typically, the first farm you set up will be a wheat farm, because these seeds are the easiest to come by in the world.

This basic farm (**Figure 7.8**) is a 9-block-by-9-block square of dirt, with a bucket of water poured into a hole in the center. It is surrounded by stone bricks with fences on top. You don't have to enclose it, but doing so makes the design of the farm look intentional and will also keep the mobs out.

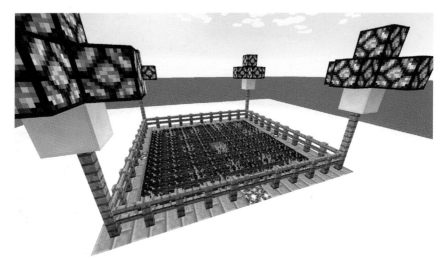

FIGURE 7.8 A basic farm pod.

To light the area, you could just place torches on top of the fence posts, but adding a little design will make your farm look better. You'll notice that the corners of the fence incorporate a version of the lampposts you saw in the previous chapter. Glowstone blocks are placed in the ground in the center of the sides.

A farm as small as this is pretty easy to harvest, but as you expand, harvesting quickly becomes tedious. Water, when allowed to flow over farmland, will wash crops away, harvesting them as if you had left-clicked each plant. This feature can be used to automate harvesting wheat, carrots, and potatoes. And if you build it correctly, the water will push your harvest to one area for easy collection.

There are a few things to keep in mind when building an automated farm. Water will flow 8 blocks, including the source, and toward a drop in terrain height. So water poured on the ground will flow over a portion of the farm and into the hole in the center (**Figure 7.9**).

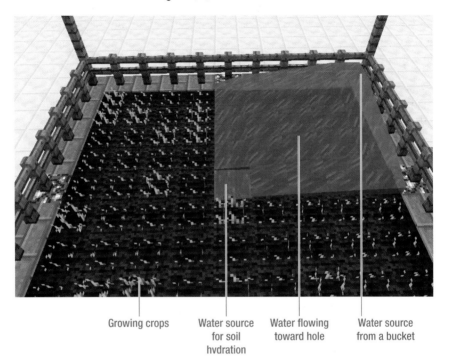

Growing crops   Water source for soil hydration   Water flowing toward hole   Water source from a bucket

FIGURE 7.9 A failed attempt to harvest a pod with fully grown wheat. Water will flow toward the hole in the center that's used to hydrate the soil instead of flowing its full distance of 7 blocks. And because the farm is 9 blocks wide by 9 blocks deep, multiple water sources would need to be used to fully harvest the pod.

Each time water falls from its initial elevation, it can flow another 8 blocks (**Figure 7.10**).

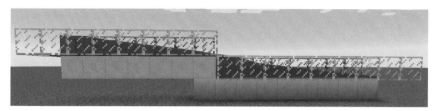

FIGURE 7.10 This side view demonstrates the way water flows. The water on the top layer flows 8 blocks. The water is allowed to drop after 7 blocks and flows another 8.

Taking these features into consideration, you can build a multi-tier farm that you can harvest by releasing water and allowing it to flow over the farm. The farm in **Figure 7.11** is two tiers tall. The bottom tier is 8 blocks deep. The top tier is 7 blocks deep and built 1 block higher than the bottom tier to allow the water to drop a level at the end. Water flows from the top to bottom along one side, hydrating the farmland 4 blocks to the right of the flow. If you place stone slabs above the water, you will be able to walk around the farm without disturbing the crops.

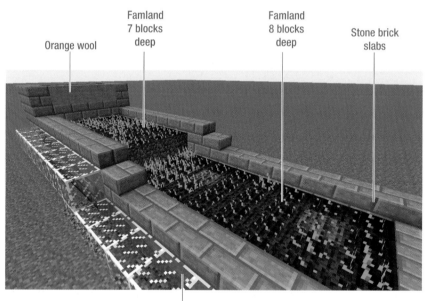

FIGURE 7.11 A multi-tier farm. Buckets of water are poured behind each orange wool block. When the orange wool is broken, water is released and allowed to flow over the farm, harvesting the crops. Stone brick slabs placed along the sides will allow you to walk up and down the farm while preventing the water from flowing outside of the farm.

When you release water over the farm, it will flow from the top to bottom, pushing all your harvest to the bottom, where you can walk along the path and collect the items. When you're ready to stop the water, place a block back in front of the water, as demonstrated in Figure 7.11 with orange wool.

Automated Farm

There are a couple of additions you can make to further automate the farm. You can completely eliminate the need to place water and break blocks to release it by crafting and placing dispensers. A dispenser spits out an item from its inventory each time it receives a redstone signal. It can also simulate placing a bucket of water (**Figure 7.12**).

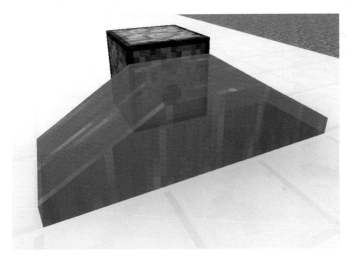

FIGURE 7.12 Demonstrating the use of dispensers to release water.

To place the dispensers, climb to the top of your farm, and with your back to the bottom, right-click to place the dispenser (crafted from seven cobblestone, one bow, and one redstone) next to the farmland. Move to the back of the dispenser, aim your reticle at the block just behind and below the dispenser, and right -click to place a redstone repeater (crafted from three stone, two redstone torches, and one redstone) (**Figure 7.13**). Do this for each dispenser. The redstone repeater, when activated by a redstone signal, will send a signal to the dispenser, causing the dispenser to dispense water.

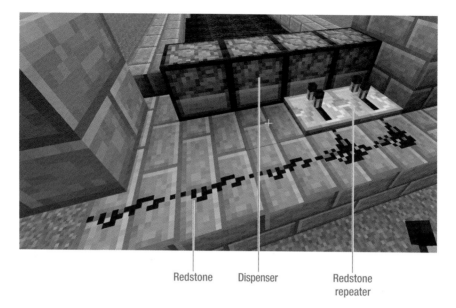

Redstone   Dispenser   Redstone
repeater

FIGURE 7.13 Demonstrating the placement of repeaters.

Place redstone dust on the block behind each repeater and 1 block to the left or right. Place 1 block of any material on top of the redstone dust that's extending out and not touching a repeater (the block you placed will look like it's floating in the air). Finally, place a button on the front face of the block (**Figure 7.14**).

Right-click each dispenser and move a bucket of water into its inventory. Right-click the button to activate it. It will send a signal to the block below. The signal will travel along the redstone dust, through the repeaters, and into the dispensers. The dispensers will dispense water. Activate the button again and the dispensers will suck the water back up.

You can utilize hoppers to collect your harvest automatically and deliver the items to a chest (**Figure 7.15**). When an item drops onto a hopper, it will be sucked into the hopper's inventory. If the hopper is attached to a chest, it will slowly deliver the items into it.

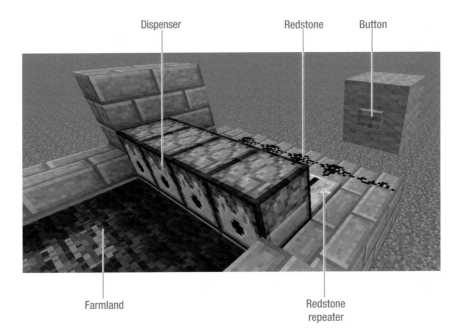

FIGURE 7.14 Proper placement of redstone repeaters, dust, and a button. Here, the redstone runs on stone bricks. The button is placed on orange wool.

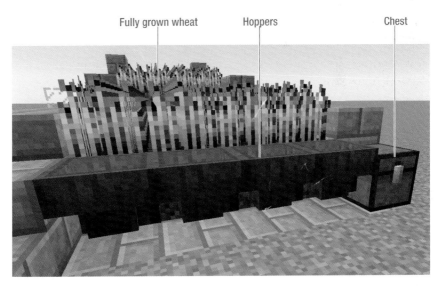

FIGURE 7.15 Hoppers and chests laid out at the bottom of the farm. Each hopper feeds into the one to the right of it, except the last one, which feeds into the chest.

Hoppers attach to the block they're placed against and won't attach to anything around it until the hopper is broken and replaced. To place a hopper against a chest or another hopper, hold the hopper in your hand, press and hold the Shift key, and right-click the side of the hopper or chest.

When your crops are fully grown (**Figure 7.16**), activate the button connected to your dispensers to allow the water to flow. When the water has pushed your harvest down to the bottom, activate the button again and the water will stop flowing, allowing you to replant. Check the chest at the bottom for your harvest.

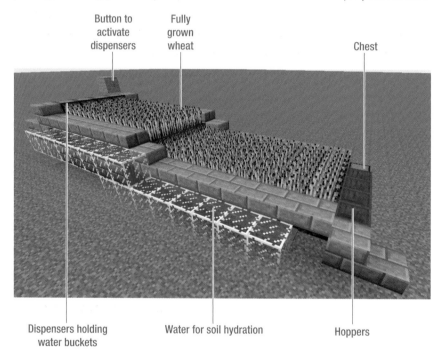

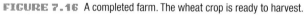

FIGURE 7.16 A completed farm. The wheat crop is ready to harvest.

Trees

Trees grow from saplings—most from a single sapling. You can plant saplings on dirt, podzol, and grass. Trees need a light level of nine in order to grow, but they do not need to be near water. When the wood from the trunk is removed from a tree, the leaf blocks start to decay and will drop saplings. Oak trees drop both saplings and apples.

Minecraft currently has six types of saplings: oak, dark oak, birch, acacia, jungle, and spruce. Generally, the more open space above the sapling, the taller the tree will grow.

- Oak trees grow from a single sapling. To grow, oak saplings need at least 5 blocks of open air directly above them. Taller oak trees have a chance to sprout branches or grow into a large oak tree.

- Dark oak grows from four dark oak saplings sown in a 2x2 square. They need at least 7 spaces of air above them to grow. Dark oak trees have a much lower sapling yield than oak. After you harvest a dark oak tree, you might not have enough saplings to grow another one. Because of this, you'll need a much larger farm to ensure sustainability.

- Birch trees grow from a single sapling. They need at least 6 blocks of air above them and do not grow branches.

- Acacia trees grow from a single sapling and need at least 7 open spaces above them. Branches sprout in the leaf canopy.

- Jungle trees grow from a single sapling and need at least 7 open spaces above. They do not sprout branches. You can grow a giant jungle tree by placing four saplings in a 2x2-block square with at least 13 blocks of air above them. A giant jungle tree grows branches and vines run down its trunk.

- Spruce trees grow from a single sapling and need at least 7 spaces of air above them and 2 blocks all around them. As with jungle trees, it's possible to grow a giant spruce tree by placing four spruce saplings in a 2x2 square. The giant spruce trees need at least 16 open blocks above them.

Tree Farm

The best tree farm to build early on is oak. Oak trees are the easiest to come by in your world, and they drop plenty of saplings. Plus, decaying leaves will sometimes drop apples, which can be eaten.

In addition to being functional, the farm you're going to build will be pleasant to visit. It will include space for 16 saplings and be easy to expand. Because of the sapling spacing used here, you can use this same design for other types of trees, including the giant versions, and yield enough saplings to sustain your farm.

To start, dig out a hole that's 16 blocks by 16 blocks by 1 block deep. Fill the outer three layers with oak wooden planks. This will be your outer path. Place a dirt block in one of the inside corners, and then place a dirt block every 2 blocks until you've placed 16 blocks of dirt inside. Fill in the remaining holes with wooden planks (**Figure 7.17**). Finally, place saplings on the dirt blocks.

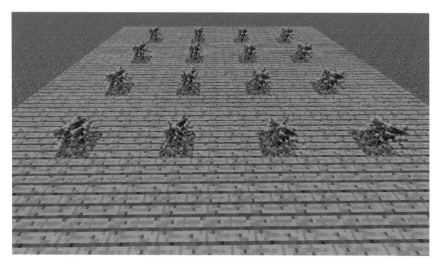

FIGURE 7.17 A basic oak tree farm.

Your choice of building material does not matter, but it's appealing to incorporate the resource you're growing into the building housing it. Later, when you expand the farm to include other types of trees, you can use their wood to add onto your farm.

While you might think that allowing your oak trees to grow large or sprout branches will result in a larger yield, it's actually a great hindrance to creating an efficient farm. Leaves won't fully decay if they're connected to a wood block, and it can be difficult to spot an individual wood block in an area dense with leaves.

The easiest way to prevent the growth of large oak trees is to simply place a block 7 to 9 blocks above where you place a sapling. Blocks at this height can become the floor of the second level of your tree farm (**Figure 7.18**). The second floor, and subsequent floors, of your farm will use the same layout as the floor below it.

FIGURE 7.18 The second level of your farm will grow birch trees. This floor is set high enough to allow some of the taller oak trees to grow while still preventing the growth of large oaks.

Lighting for the Farm

You could just place torches on the ground to keep your farm lit up, but that makes lighting look like an afterthought. Instead, use recessed lighting with torches in the floor of the first level and glowstone blocks in the floor of the second and subsequent levels (**Figure 7.19**). The glowstone blocks will provide additional light to the room below.

FIGURE 7.19 A fully lit tree farm. Some saplings have grown into trees. The first level is enclosed on three sides with glass panes and edged with stone bricks.

Cactus for Green Dye

Cactus grows naturally in the desert and mesa biomes, but you can farm it in any biome. Cactus, when cooked in a furnace, will turn into cactus green, which can be used to dye wool, hardened clay, or glass. It can be used in fireworks or combined with lapis lazuli to make cyan dye or combined with bonemeal to make lime dye.

Cactus does not grow from seeds. Instead, place a cactus block on sand and wait. It will grow 3 blocks tall. Each block of the plant can then be placed on sand and will grow into a new plant.

However, cactus cannot touch a block on any side.

If growing cactus encounters a block on any side, the cactus block that touches another block will break off. This feature allows you to automate a cactus farm.

First, place a rectangle of blocks (any solid building material, such as stone bricks, will work) 9 blocks wide by 9 blocks deep. Build a 1-block-tall wall around on the sides and the back of the platform (**Figure 7.20**).

FIGURE 7.20 The base of the cactus farm.

Next, 3 blocks from the left side and 3 blocks from the back, build a 2-block-tall pillar of stone brick blocks. There should be 2 blocks of open space between the left and back walls and the pillar. Build another pillar from stone bricks. There should be 1 block of open air between the 2 pillars and 2 blocks of open air between the right wall and the back. Build a 5-block-tall pillar between the 2 already there.

Break the bottom 4 blocks on the middle pillar and the bottom block on the pillars to the left and right. You should now have 3 floating blocks (**Figure 7.21**).

FIGURE 7.21 On the left is the structure you'll have after you construct the pillars. On the right is the base of the pillars that have been removed.

Place 1 block of sand on each of the two lower floating blocks and then a cactus on top of the sand. When the cactus grows, the top cactus block will break off and fall below.

But standing around and waiting for the cactus to break isn't any fun, so you're going to automate the collection. Pour buckets of water on the floor, against the back wall. The water should all flow in the same direction.

As you did for the crop farm, place a chest in front of and 1 block to the right of the platform. Place a hopper so it connects to the chest, and then, moving to the left, place six more so they're all connected (**Figure 7.22**).

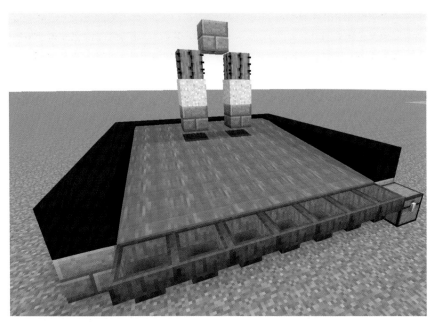

FIGURE 7.22 A fully automated cactus farm.

Now, when the cactus grows and breaks off, the water will push your harvest to the hoppers. The cactus will move through the hoppers and end up in the chest at the end. You can expand this farm by placing four more cactus pads in front of the two already in place or by expanding the base structure to accommodate even more pads. Be sure to leave 1 block of open air between cactus pads.

Mining

Mining is an integral part of Minecraft—much of what you can craft and build depends on what you mine. When mining in the overworld, you'll find materials you can use for building; metals you can use for tools, armor, and rails, among other things; and redstone dust you can use for elaborate contraptions. You can use coal as fuel in furnaces and powered mine carts or as a crafting ingredient for fire charges used in fireworks, or you can craft it into a block of coal. You'll also find gravel, which has a chance of dropping flint when dug up with a shovel. Flint is used in the crafting of arrows and an item called "flint and steel" (hold "flint and steel" in your hand and right-click a block to start a fire). You'll also find gems like diamonds (which are used in a number of crafting recipes, including tools and armor) and emeralds (which can be traded with villagers).

When mining in the Nether, you'll encounter nether quartz and gravel. The most common block in the Nether is netherrack, which, when lit with flint and steel, will burn indefinitely. You'll also find soul sand. Mobs and players move more slowly than normal when walking over soul sand. Nether wart, an ingredient in potions, grows only on soul sand. Glowstone, which is useful for lighting, appears in clusters on the ceiling of the Nether.

Ores, such as iron and gold, are generated in the world at varying levels. The key to an efficient and successful mining trip is to get to the depth of the ore for which you are hunting as quickly as possible. The optimal level for mining is level 11. This will give you access to all of the ores in reasonable concentrations and still keep you (mostly) above the lava pools.

To find your current level, press the F3 key on your keyboard to bring up a debug screen. In the upper-left corner of the screen you should see a bunch of numbers (**Figure 7.23**). The number labeled Y is your vertical position in the world.

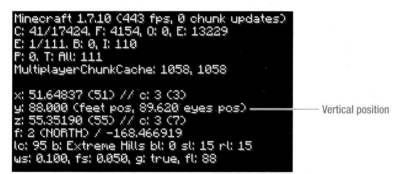

FIGURE 7.23 Y is your vertical position in the world. Here, the player is standing at level 88. Your eyes will always be slightly higher. When looking for a certain elevation, you should be looking at where you're standing.

There are three main techniques for mining, with slight variations on each: spelunking (or caving), shaft mining, and branch mining. No matter which technique you choose, always be sure you have torches in your inventory.

Spelunking

Spelunking is simply the exploration of caves or cave systems. Caves (**Figure 7.24**) are a primary feature of a Minecraft world. You'll encounter cave entrances on the surface or while mining or carving out a home. As you explore, mine any ores you see exposed. It's important to bring torches, extra food, and an extra set of tools with you. As you mine, your tools will become damaged until they eventually break. Caves are quite dark, and it's very easy to get lost in a large cave system. In addition to lighting a cave as you go, torches can be used to help you find your way back. An often-used technique is to place torches on the wall to your left as you go. When you're ready to head back to the surface, follow the cave system, keeping the torches on your right side.

FIGURE 7.24 A fully lit cave with exposed iron ore on the far left and gold ore in the bottom.

When exploring, you'll likely encounter a branch of a cave system that you're not ready to explore. If you leave it unlit and exposed to the area you've already explored, you run the risk of having hostile mobs wander out of the darkness. The easiest way to deal with this is to make an X with blocks and place torches on the X (**Figure 7.25**). Not only will this stop mobs from wandering, but it's a signal that you have an unexplored branch.

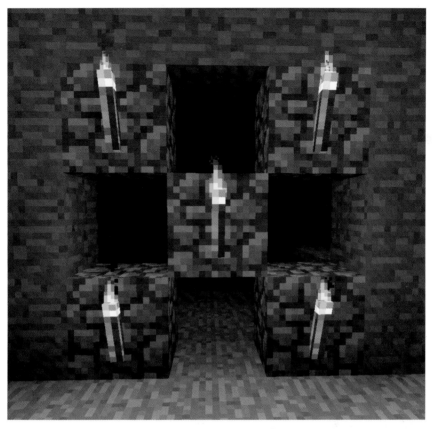

FIGURE 7.25 A cave branch, temporarily blocked by cobblestone.

Shaft Mining

Shaft mining is basically drilling straight down to bedrock, mining any ores or pockets of ore you encounter. One of the fundamental tenets of Minecraft is "Never dig straight down!" It's possibly the most dangerous method. It's hard to get out of the way if you expose lava even if you place ladders as you go. You also run the risk of digging straight through the ceiling of a cave system— taking damage from falling, being attacked by mobs that may be hiding in the cave, or falling straight into a pool of lava. But there are ways to make it a little bit safer.

Be sure you have enough ladders in your inventory to reach from the top of your chute to the level you're digging to. Find a spot to start digging down, and stand in the middle of 2 blocks. Aim your reticle down, and mine the left block (**Figure 7.26**). The right block will continue holding you up. Mine the right block and you'll drop down a level. Choose one side of the hole to place a ladder, and then place one on the wall.

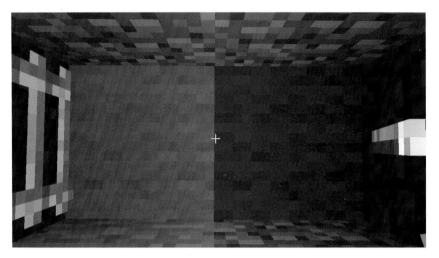

FIGURE 7.26 Alternating between mining the block you're standing on and the one next to it should increase the safety of this method. On the left is a ladder; on the right is a torch.

Each time you dig a level, place another ladder on the wall below the previous one (**Figure 7.27**). Every few blocks, place a torch on the wall opposite the ladders. Continue alternating mining and placing ladders and torches until you reach the level you're aiming for. Alternating between mining the left and right blocks should allow you to stop before you mine straight into a cavern.

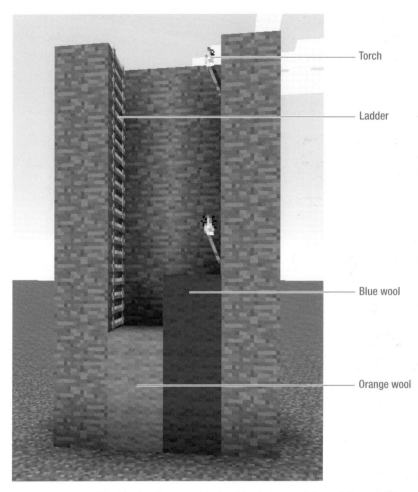

Torch

Ladder

Blue wool

Orange wool

FIGURE 7.27 This side view demonstrates alternating between mining and placing ladders and torches. The orange and blue wool blocks demonstrate where you'll be digging.

Head back to the surface, leave 2 blocks of unmined material between the hole you've just dug and the new hole (**Figure 7.28**), and repeat the process.

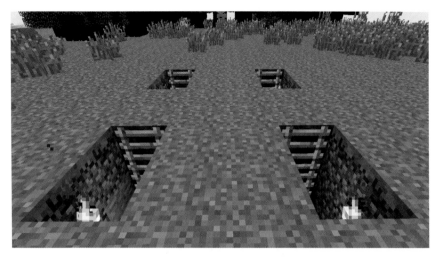

FIGURE 7.28 Leaving 2 blocks of space between the holes ensures you expose all surfaces, without having to mine extra.

Branch Mining

Branch mining allows you to reach a desirable level quickly and mine materials with less danger than shaft mining. You first carve a staircase or dig a shaft to the level you'd like to mine (level 11 is most efficient, but any level works). If you've dug a shaft down to the level, you'll find it tedious to climb up and down the ladder each time you need to transfer materials between the surface and your mine. While you can't avoid having to climb up the ladder, you can build a drop chute.

To build a drop chute, dig a 2-block-wide tunnel straight down, as if you were shaft mining. Place ladders on one side of the shaft as you dig down. Suspend water at the bottom (**Figure 7.29**).

Water flow can be stopped by placing blocks, but you need to be able to fall all the way through the water. Use a sign instead; it will stop the water but won't stop you from falling.

When you want to get to the bottom, simply jump in the hole. Ordinarily, falling from a great height will kill you. However, falling through water will slow you down enough that you don't take any damage.

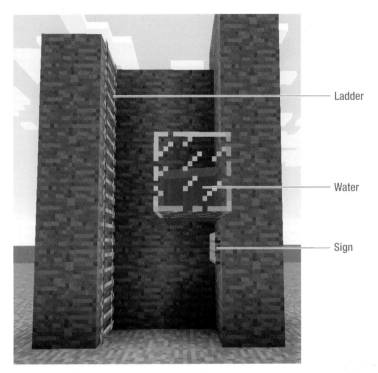

Ladder

Water

Sign

FIGURE 7.29 A cutaway side view of the bottom of a drop chute.

Once the drop chute is completed, carve out a room that's 10 blocks wide by 10 blocks deep by 4 blocks high. Initially, this will give you enough space to place some chests and a furnace or two.

Pick any direction and mine out a tunnel or branch that's 1 block wide by 2 blocks high by 11 blocks deep. Place a torch at the entrance and a torch on the ground at the end of the branch.

Two blocks to the left or right of the tunnel you've just dug, place a torch on the ground, mine another branch with the same dimensions as the first, and place another torch at the end (**Figure 7.30**).

When you're ready to start on another level, dig out a staircase up to the second level above the floor. Start your branching 1 block to the left or right of the tunnels below (**Figure 7.31**), and then follow the same spacing pattern as the first level.

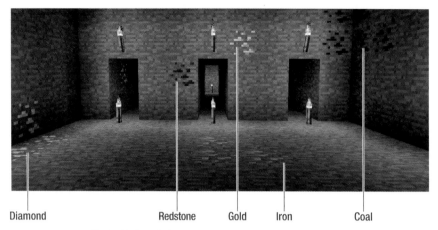

Diamond   Redstone   Gold   Iron   Coal

FIGURE 7.30 The beginning of a branch mine. Your branches can be as deep as you'd like, but following the width, height, and spacing pattern will ensure that you expose as much ore as possible.

FIGURE 7.31 Adding onto the branch mine. The second level is offset by 1 block in order to expose more ore. The staircase is demonstrated by orange wool on the left.

Summary

In Minecraft, your creativity is limited only by the materials you can gather. Take advantage of the techniques described in this chapter and there will be no limits on what you can build. Automated farms and efficient mines will help you spend less time gathering materials and more time working on your masterpiece.

Putting It All Together

Whether you're building a small hut or a colossal castle, the process of designing, building, and furnishing your creation is very satisfying. Experimenting with different shapes, adding depth, playing with color, and varying materials can make even the simplest structure a work of art.

Breaking a complex structure down into simple shapes is a great way to figure out how to replicate it. A standard house might be a cuboid with a triangular roof. The drum towers of medieval castles, lighthouses, and submarines are all, at their most basic, cylinders.

Creating Shapes

Even though the Minecraft world is made up of square blocks, you can still make circular shapes (**Figure 8.1**).

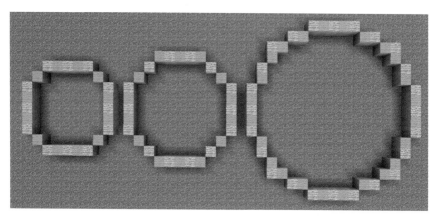

FIGURE 8.1 The circular shape on the left is 9 blocks in diameter. The shape in the middle is 11 blocks and the shape on the right is 17 blocks. In this example, the alternating orange and light blue wool blocks help you count the blocks.

While you can attempt to make a circle through trial and error, a number of people have created tools that eliminate the guesswork. An online search for "Minecraft circle generator" will turn up pages of generators and tips. The Pixel Circle/Oval Generator, located at donatstudios.com/PixelCircleGenerator, allows you to set a length and width, gives the option to generate a thick border (the edges will have more blocks), and gives you a block count. This tool tells you that a circle with a diameter of 11, for example, will require 28 blocks.

Stacking circular shapes will give you a cylinder and the start of a watchtower (**Figure 8.2**).

FIGURE 8.2 The beginnings of a watchtower. Stone brick is used as the base material. The tower is 11 blocks in diameter and 11 blocks tall.

To add a main viewing platform to your watchtower, build a 1-block-tall circular shape 17 blocks in diameter on top of the base tower. Around the edge, place fences. And on top of the platform, build a circular shape 9 blocks in diameter and 6 blocks tall (**Figure 8.3**). You can leave the ceiling of the upper portion of the tower completely open, but the tower will look and feel incomplete. Glass blocks are a good choice for the ceiling because they allow sunlight in.

Once the basic shape of the structure is in place, go back and remove blocks where you'd like your door and windows. The window on the base of the watchtower uses fences and the window on top uses glass panes, but you can use any combination.

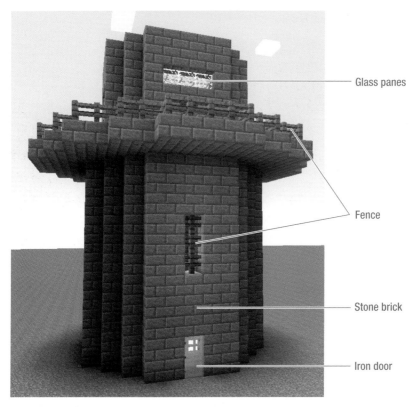

Glass panes

Fence

Stone brick

Iron door

FIGURE 8.3 The mostly completed watchtower. Adding fences to the windows in the walls gives the illusion of lookout points. Glass panes make windows in the top section. And of course, doors are included.

Varying Materials

Varying the materials you use will keep your structures looking fresh. The Cape Cod–style house you saw in Chapter 5, "There's No Place Like Home," looks fine, but it could look better. Upgrade the materials in the main structure to give it a boost (**Figure 8.4**).

Dark oak wood stairs

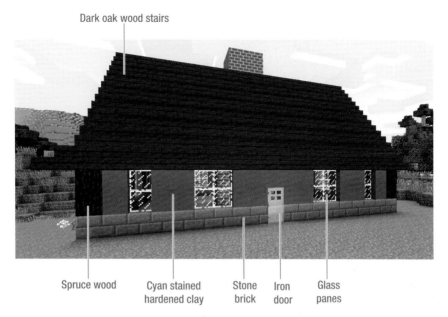

Spruce wood   Cyan stained   Stone   Iron   Glass
hardened clay   brick   door   panes

FIGURE 8.4 The foundation of the house has been made with stone bricks. The walls are now cyan-stained hardened clay. Instead of oak wood stairs, the roof is now dark oak wood stairs. Spruce wood has been added to corners to give the house a little more depth and variation.

You can use cobblestone for pathways, but they'll look more interesting if you use a different material (**Figure 8.5**). Stone bricks are a versatile building material suitable for everything from foundations and walls to pathways.

FIGURE 8.5 Stone bricks used for a path.

Adding Depth

Adding depth to your structures will make them more visually interesting, and the design will look more intentional. Trapdoors are one way to add a layer of depth. Use them on a house to imitate shutters (**Figure 8.6**), or on glowstone or redstone lamps to add visual interest.

FIGURE 8.6 Trapdoors used as shutters. The lamppost to the right is built by stacking two nether brick fences end to end and then placing a glowstone block on top. Trapdoors are placed on the four sides of the glowstone block to give it more depth.

Let's revisit the pathway to your house. You could mix in some cracked stone brick blocks to make it look well trodden, or instead of just varying the pattern, you could change the height of your path. You can imitate an edged path by using slabs that are half the height of regular blocks, with stairs on either side (**Figure 8.7**).

To build this type of path, start by digging out a hole that's 3 blocks wide by 6 blocks long by 1 block deep. You can, of course, make your path as long as you need it. Place your slabs along the middle of the hole until the center is covered (**Figure 8.8**).

Standing on the middle slab, face one of the sides of your path and place your stairs on the ground in the hole (**Figure 8.9**). When you're finished with one side, turn to face the opposite side and repeat the process.

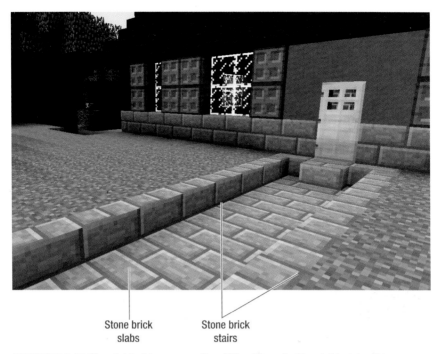

Stone brick
slabs

Stone brick
stairs

FIGURE 8.7 Stone brick slabs compose the middle of the path. Stone brick stairs sit on either side.

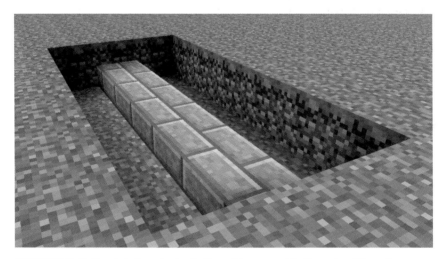

FIGURE 8.8 The start of an edged path. Stone slabs are used for the center of the walkway.

FIGURE 8.9 One side of the path completed.

Walls, like paths, benefit from adding depth. The wall in **Figure 8.10** is 5 blocks tall and constructed from cobblestone.

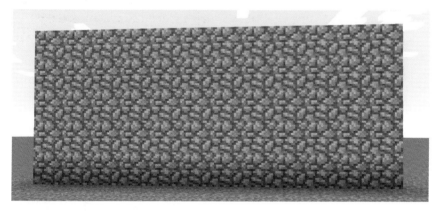

FIGURE 8.10 A bland wall.

Introducing a second building material to the wall will make it look a little more interesting (**Figure 8.11**), but it still doesn't quite feel complete.

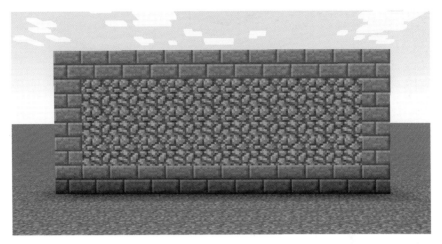

FIGURE 8.11 Stone bricks have replaced the cobblestone blocks around the edge.

To give this wall some depth, place stone brick stairs as you normally would on the ground in front of the bottom row of stone bricks. In front of the column of stone bricks on either side, place another column of stone bricks (**Figure 8.12**). Then place stairs upside down on the face of the top row of stone bricks. To place stairs upside down, hold stairs in your hand, aim your reticle at the upper half of the face of a block you want to place the stair block against, and right-click. If your stairs don't appear to be upside down, break them and try it again, but aim your reticle slightly higher.

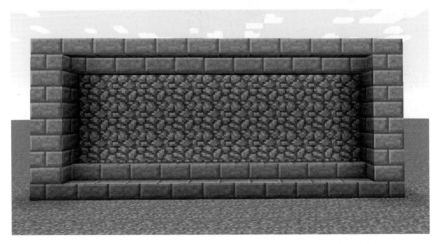

FIGURE 8.12 This wall, constructed from cobblestone, stone bricks, and stone brick stairs, looks much more interesting than a wall constructed solely of cobblestone.

Going Further

Once you've mastered these basic techniques you'll be ready to move on to some elaborate and unique structures. Add to your courtyards a fountain that is not only ornate but doubles as a monument, install working lighthouses at your docks, and much more.

The monument in **Figure 8.13** takes advantage of flowing water to give it a unique look.

FIGURE 8.13 Monuments don't have to resemble anything in particular.

Lighthouses can be constructed in many shapes and sizes. The sides can reach straight up or taper near the top. They can stand by themselves or have a house attached to one side. The lighthouse in **Figure 8.14** uses a basic cylinder for its shape.

FIGURE 8.14 This lighthouse alternates red stained clay blocks and quartz blocks in a spiral pattern to give it a traditional look.

Iron bars are placed around the outside of the observatory. The redstone lamps in the observatory are wired to a daylight sensor. The lights will turn on at night and off during the day.

Summary

Throughout history, people have built structures with the materials they've had available. As technology progressed and civilizations grew, different types of materials were available. To a large degree, the same will happen in Minecraft. Your first house will be composed of basic materials and will likely be small. As you're able to mine faster with better tools and take greater risks with better weapons and armor, you'll acquire better materials and more of them. The examples shown here will give you a starting point, but don't limit yourself to one source. Draw inspiration from real-life structures, architectural styles, architects, interior designers, or other Minecraft players. If you're still looking for inspiration, an online search can be very helpful. When you have an idea, spend a little time researching, put in some effort, and you'll find a way to realize it in the Minecraft world.

PART 4

REDSTONE

One of Minecraft's more complex and interesting aspects is redstone. At its most basic, redstone allows you to place a lever or a pressure plate to open a door. At its most complex, redstone allows players to create working calculators and massive automated constructions. From locking doors to hidden traps to machines that can be "programmed" to play songs, the possibilities are endless.

We'll explore exactly what redstone is, how we can use it, and all the tools that are part of working with redstone. We'll also look at some projects, breaking them down step by step, so that you can see redstone in action. Soon you'll be using redstone with ease!

Redstone Power

Get ready, you're going to learn all about redstone—how to find and mine it, what you can use it for, and the craftable components that you can use to make circuits. At the end of the section, you'll find some projects that you can try for yourself, from simple lamps and locked doors to cannons and firework launchers.

Learning to craft with redstone can be tricky, but with patience and practice you'll build all sorts of devices. Everyone learns in different ways. Some people like to follow step-by-step directions and see how things are put together bit by bit, while others prefer to experiment and try things on their own. You might find that you learn best in one of those ways, or you, like most people, may have lots of ways to learn new things.

As you'll soon see, there are endless ways to design with redstone.

So What Is Redstone?

Redstone is an ore that you can mine. It's pretty easy to find (it even glows a little bit when it or the surrounding blocks are mined). When you mine it, it breaks into redstone dust (unless you're using a Silk Touch pick, which will leave it in its original form), which you can also craft into redstone blocks (**Figure 9.1**).

FIGURE 9.1 Redstone ore, dust, and block.

You can use redstone dust in potions to make them last longer. You can also use it to craft a couple of items: clocks and compasses. But its main use is in redstone circuits.

Redstone circuitry is the Minecraft version of electricity. When you place redstone dust on blocks, they become powered blocks (they conduct electricity, but you can touch them without being hurt). You'll find that most blocks can become powered blocks, but some—such as glass, ice, and leaves—cannot, and neither can stairs or slabs. Redstone blocks (crafted from redstone) are powered without needing dust laid on them.

Using powered blocks, you can make paths for the redstone power to follow. When you add special items, such as switches, buttons, or repeaters, you can turn that redstone power on and off, allowing you to make all sorts of cool powered devices.

Mining for Redstone

Redstone ore usually occurs in veins (**Figure 9.2**), which means you'll find several blocks together. It is found only deep underground, at level 16 and lower, and it glows red in the dark when it, or the blocks around it, are disturbed.

FIGURE 9.2 Mining for redstone.

You can mine redstone with any pick, but unless you are using an iron or diamond pick, you won't get any redstone dust from the ore. Using a wooden or stone pick will just break the block, leaving you nothing for your hard work.

If you use a regular iron or diamond pick, you'll get four or five pieces of dust from each ore. But if you mine it with a Fortune-enchanted pick, you'll get extra redstone—with the amount you gain dependent on the level of your enchant. If you have a Silk Touch enchant on your pick, the ore will stay in the same form as when you mine it. Smelting a redstone ore block will only give you one piece of redstone, so it makes more sense to mine it.

Crafting with Redstone

You can use a crafting table to craft redstone blocks from redstone dust (**Figure 9.3**). Not only are blocks helpful in building devices, but they make great decorative blocks for building and make it easier to stack and store.

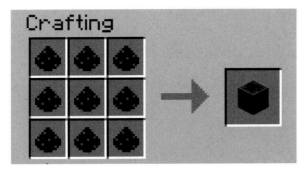

FIGURE 9.3 The recipe for crafting redstone blocks is very straightforward.

Many items that you can make on a crafting table use redstone as part of the recipe. Two of these are game items that aren't used in redstone circuitry: clocks and compasses.

Clocks (**Figure 9.4**) are made with gold ingots and redstone. They don't keep the exact time but can tell day from night. They are handy to have when you are deep underground and can't tell if it is dark on the surface. You can also place a clock in an item frame to make a working wall clock.

You can make a compass (**Figure 9.5**) in the same way as a clock, but using iron ingots and redstone. A compass will always point toward your original spawn point. Even if you've used a bed to create a new spawn point, the compass will point to your original spawn point.

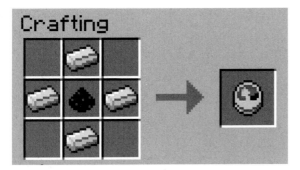

FIGURE 9.4 Clock recipe: gold ingots and redstone dust.

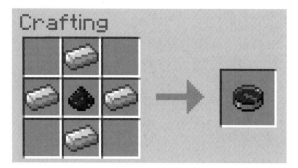

FIGURE 9.5 Compass recipe: iron ingots and redstone dust.

Compasses are most often used to make blank maps, from which you make maps of an area you are in. When maps are placed in item frames, they completely cover the face of the block, allowing you to make wall maps of a large area or to use maps as decoration or a form of wallpaper.

Redstone Circuitry

Redstone circuitry can be as simple as a redstone lamp or as complex as a locking door that uses a jukebox for the lock and a specific disc for the key. No matter the size of the project, the basic principles of redstone circuits don't change.

Redstone power (or simply power) travels along a path or line. It can be straight or crooked. When a line of redstone dust is laid down, it is sometimes called redstone wire. It needs a power source, such a redstone torch, switch, or repeater (more on these later).

Redstone can usually transmit power for 15 blocks before it fades out completely (this is less for some devices, like daylight sensors). When it is powered, it is brightly lit. The farther it is from the power source, the darker it becomes (**Figure 9.6**), losing one measure of intensity per block.

FIGURE 9.6 Redstone power decreases by one with each block.

Before we go further into how circuits work, let's look at the components, how to craft them, and what they do.

Redstone Switches

Many types of switches can be used with redstone. Some, such as buttons and pressure plates, must be held to activate the current. These turn off when released, whereas others, such as levers, can stay in an on or off position.

Redstone Torch

A redstone torch (**Figure 9.7**) is a power source for redstone. Like a regular torch, it can be placed on the top or side of a block. It provides continuous power to redstone that is beside or above the torch. If you want to be able to turn the power on and off, you need to use a switch, like a lever or button. Redstone torches are used in a few redstone recipes.

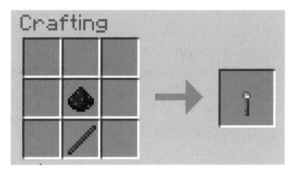

FIGURE 9.7 Redstone torch recipe: stick and redstone.

Redstone torches can be used for lighting, like a torch, but they give off less light and mobs can spawn in the area, so be careful.

Buttons

Buttons (**Figure 9.8**), made from wood or stone, are a type of switch used with redstone. When you push a button, it activates whatever it is connected to, but the power lasts only a short while before the button resets: 1 second for stone and 1.5 seconds for wood.

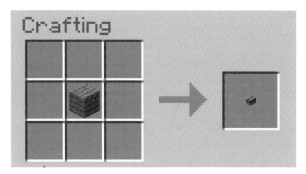

FIGURE 9.8 Button recipe: wood or smooth stone.

As of version 1.8, buttons can be placed on all sides of a block, including floors and ceilings. If an arrow strikes a wooden button, it will stay activated until the arrow is removed or despawns.

You can also use buttons as decoration in builds to add texture to blocks.

Pressure Plates

Another type of switch is a pressure plate (**Figure 9.9**). Made from wood or stone, they are activated by stepping on them. The weight of a player will press down the plate and power the redstone next to the plate. Mobs can also activate pressure plates. As soon as you step off the pressure plate, it deactivates.

As with buttons, you can use pressure plates for decoration, such as tables or countertops.

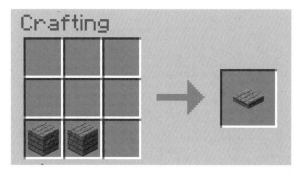

FIGURE 9.9 Pressure plate recipe: wood or smooth stone.

Weighted Pressure Plates

Like regular pressure plates, weighted pressure plates (**Figure 9.10**), made from gold or iron, act as a power source to blocks beside them. Unlike wood or stone plates, the amount of power they can emit changes depending upon the number of items or creatures on them. The signal strength for a gold weighted pressure plate increases by one intensity level for each item on it (the items must be different), or for each creature on it (it can count multiple numbers of the same mob). The signal strength of an iron plate increases by one intensity level for every 10 individual items or creatures on it.

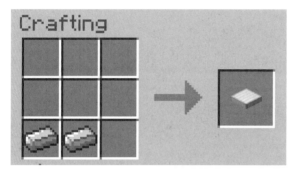

FIGURE 9.10 Weighted pressure plate recipe: iron or gold.

Levers

Levers (**Figure 9.11**) are switches that can be turned on or off. They don't rely on pressure or pushing a button, and they will stay on once activated until they are turned off.

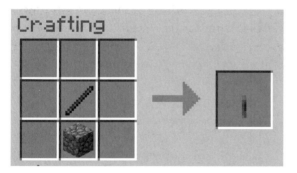

FIGURE 9.11 Lever recipe: cobblestone and stick.

You can place levers on walls, floors, and ceilings, making them more versatile than some of the other switches.

Tripwire Hooks

Tripwire hooks (**Figure 9.12**), when used in pairs with string (which is called *tripwire* when connecting two hooks), work much like pressure plates. When a player or mob moves or breaks the string (or tripwire) that connects two hooks, both hooks activate. They can stretch up to 40 blocks and are hard to see, making them perfect for traps. Players can avoid this trap if they see it and cut the tripwire with shears.

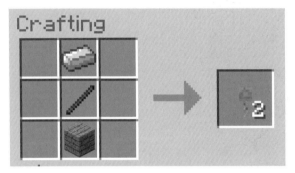

FIGURE 9.12 Tripwire hook recipe: iron ingot, stick, and wood block.

Tripwire hooks are great for decorating. They make a good gas pedal in a car or a faucet for a sink.

Daylight Sensor

A daylight sensor (**Figure 9.13**) is a type of switch that activates when the sun is in the sky. It provides energy that is dependent upon how much light there is—more in the middle of the day, less at dawn and dusk. You can use it as a timer or as a light-activated switch.

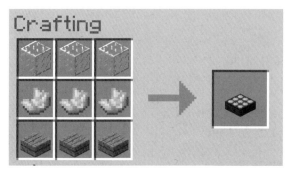

FIGURE 9.13 Daylight sensor recipe: glass, nether quartz, and wooden slabs.

Detector Rail

A detector rail (**Figure 9.14**) is much like a pressure plate for minecarts.

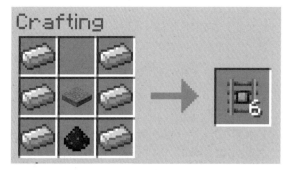

FIGURE 9.14 Detector rail recipe: iron ingot, stone pressure plate, and redstone.

Redstone Components

Many types of redstone components other than switches are available. You have plenty of options for your circuitry, from dispensers and hoppers (which help you move and distribute items) to repeaters and comparators (which move the redstone energy within the circuit).

Redstone Repeaters

Redstone repeaters (**Figure 9.15**) are used in a variety of ways: to boost the signal past the first 15 blocks that redstone wire normally can transmit energy, to delay or lock signals, and to control the direction of the signal.

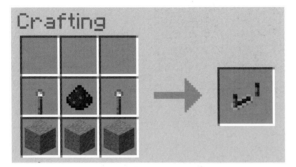

FIGURE 9.15 Redstone repeater recipe: redstone, redstone torch, and stone.

Redstone Comparators

Comparators (**Figure 9.16**) are similar to repeaters but more complex and with more uses. Comparators have two inputs and one output. They can run in one of two modes: subtraction and comparison.

You can use comparators as a measuring tool. They can tell how many items are in a chest or hopper and display the amount by producing energy that represents it (marked by how many blocks the power extends). They can also compare and use energy from both inputs or decrease the amount of energy by subtracting one from the other, depending on the setting.

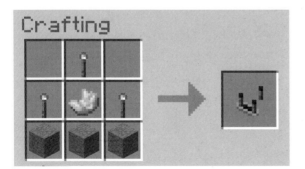

FIGURE 9.16 Comparator recipe: nether quartz, redstone torch, and stone.

Pistons

Pistons (**Figure 9.17**) can push most blocks, but they can't push obsidian, chests, or hoppers. They are activated by redstone and will extend a plate to push an adjacent block. Sticky pistons (**Figure 9.18**) are able to pull a block toward them. Pistons will break items, such as crops, redstone, and tripwires, that are on the ground.

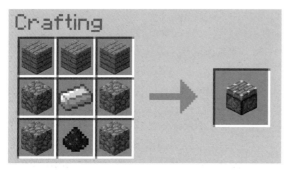

FIGURE 9.17 Piston recipe: wood, cobblestone, iron, and redstone.

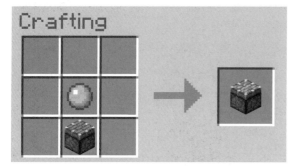

FIGURE 9.18 Sticky piston recipe: piston and slime ball.

Droppers

Droppers (**Figure 9.19**) drop items when activated. If you put a container, like a chest, in front of a dropper, it will move items into the chest or container when it's activated.

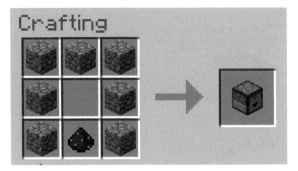

FIGURE 9.19 Dropper recipe: cobblestone and redstone.

Dispensers

Dispensers (**Figure 9.20**) are similar to droppers, but they can shoot objects, such as arrows or fireworks, a good distance. When dispensing other items, the dispenser usually propels them three blocks forward. They don't deposit into containers in the manner that droppers do. They react differently depending upon what they're dropping, such as creating water or lava source blocks from buckets of water or lava, or firing arrows.

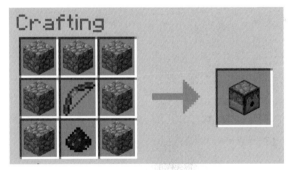

FIGURE 9.20 Dispenser recipe: cobblestone, redstone, and bow.

Hopper

A hopper (**Figure 9.21**) is a funnel-shaped block that also moves items. Items can be collected in a hopper and then automatically moved into chests or other containers. You can use a redstone signal to stop hoppers from dispensing items. Automated systems, such as farms or brewing stands, often use hoppers.

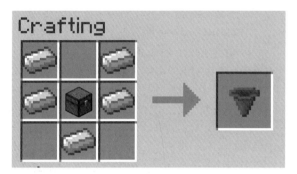

FIGURE 9.21 Hopper recipe: five iron ingots and a chest.

Currents and Circuits

Redstone circuits are not nearly as complicated as electrical circuits can be, but you can still make some pretty amazing devices and machines, especially when you add extras like switches, repeaters, and comparators. Knowing a bit about how currents and circuits work will help you when you're experimenting with redstone.

A *circuit* is the path that electricity or energy runs on between two or more points. We often call this energy the current. With redstone, a circuit includes a power source, such as a torch or lever, and the device it is operating, such as a sticky piston or a door. Redstone does not actually need to be part of the circuit, though it is more often than not.

All circuits, whether they are electrical or redstone, need two things: a power source and a connected circuit. Without power, there is no current and nothing will happen, just like when the power goes out in your house. If you don't have power, your redstone won't work.

Minecraft power sources can be redstone torches or redstone blocks, but switches such as buttons or levers are also power sources. This is different from electricity, where switches are used only to turn power on and off and are not the source of the power itself.

A circuit is a combination of a power source, wires, and components such as switches. All the parts of a circuit need to be connected to each other—there can't be places where the power doesn't flow from one part of the circuit to the next. The wires need to be connected to the power source and to the device that is being powered, as well as to any switches.

A real-life example of this is using a battery to light up a light bulb. Maybe you've done this science experiment yourself (and maybe you've even tried it with a lemon or potato instead of a battery!). To make a closed circuit, we connect two wires to the two ends of the battery. Without something for the wires to connect to, there isn't a circuit, but if we attach those ends to a light bulb, the power can flow from the battery to the bulb and back to the battery, making a circuit.

Redstone circuits are a little different—we can send the power from the source, such as a redstone torch, to the device we want to power, like a redstone lamp, without using a second wire to go back to the torch or even having a wire. A redstone circuit can be as simple as placing a lever on a redstone lamp (**Figure 9.22**). Once we start to add other parts, the circuit can become much more complex.

FIGURE 9.22 A redstone lamp can be powered on and off by a lever attached directly to it.

Power On, Power Off

With all circuits, power is either on or off. There is no in-between. In Minecraft, we usually say that redstone is powered (on) or unpowered (off).

Sometimes we don't want the power to always be turned on, and that is when we use switches. We use switches such as buttons, levers, and pressure plates to power the redstone on or off in the same way that you might flip your light switch to turn your lamp on or off.

Going back to our battery and light bulb example, we might not want to detach the wire (open the circuit) every time we want to turn the light off. We can add a simple switch, like a light switch. A switch lets us stop the flow of electricity from the battery to the bulb. A switch in Minecraft does the same thing to redstone power.

In Minecraft, switches can also be used as power sources, not just as a way to turn power on and off. For example, pushing a button will create a burst of power that lasts one to one and a half seconds, while pressure plates provide power as long as there is something weighing them down.

The location of switches and powered blocks makes a difference. Most blocks, except some like glass, leaves, stairs, and slabs, can be turned into a powered block. Once a block is powered it can share that power with any of the blocks around it, but different switches can change how that works. Some items, like redstone torches, buttons, pressure plates, and levers, actually power the block they are in, which is simply an empty air block, the space the button or lever extends into, as well as the block that they are attached to. For instance, pressure plates power the block they are placed on, which is under them, while a button will power the block it is on as well as the block it is physically in.

The dynamics of this power changes when redstone wire is added—it can change whether a block or source is on or off, as can additional switches. It is important to experiment with these items and redstone and learn how various switches and blocks are powered and work together.

Input and Output

When power is going into a device we call it an *input*, and when it comes from a device we call it an *output*.

With our light bulb, the power coming from the battery to the bulb is the input, and the light turning on is the output.

In Minecraft, input and output take two forms, either powered or unpowered. Another way to look at the different systems for input and output is called logic gates.

Logic Gates

Logic gates are not gates at all. As a matter of fact, they aren't even objects or items. A logic gate is a basic electrical system or device (or, in Minecraft, a redstone system or device) that makes logical decisions based on input or combinations of input that are part of its design. Each logic gate is just a collection of components that are put together in a specific way to create a circuit that functions according to certain rules. They can be very confusing, but the more you use them, the more you'll understand their uses.

Logic gates are an important part of how electronic devices and computers work. You may have already studied them in science. Minecraft logic gates are the same as those used in electronics and computers. There are many different types of gates with simple names that pretty much explain how they function, such as AND, OR, NOT, NOR, and NAND gates. Each gate always functions in exactly the same way, so if you know what you want a circuit to do and you know the different logic gates, you already know the basics.

The most basic gate is a block with a switch, which is the input, and redstone dust or a simple device, the output. Putting a lever onto a redstone lamp, as in Figure 9.22, for example, is a basic gate, where you turn the power on or off for a direct result. You can extend the line between the input and output, by adding a line of redstone between the lever and the redstone lamp (**Figure 9.23**), but it still is a simple input/output gate.

Logic gates give us a lot more control over what we can do with redstone, because they help us control the way the power moves through the circuit.

This sounds pretty complicated, but let's think about our example with the light bulb. What if we had two switches on our light bulb instead of just one? Let's call them switch A and switch B.

If we had to turn both switches on for the bulb to light up, we would call that an AND circuit, because both A *and* B need to be on.

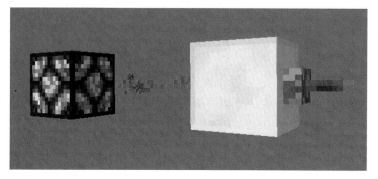

FIGURE 9.23 Simple input/output gate.

If the bulb lit up with just one switch turned on, we would call that an OR circuit, because either switch A *or* switch B can be turned on for light bulb to work.

In both cases, we can use logic gates to make circuits work the way that we want them to. We can do the same thing in Minecraft with our redstone circuits. We can use our redstone circuits to understand logic gates.

Logic gates are all about input and output. Using switches and different components allows each gate to work in a very specific way, and there are rules for how you create each type of gate. Different gates are helpful for different tasks. For instance, if you want to make a light that is activated by a daylight sensor to turn on at night, knowing how to make a NOT gate is useful.

Here, we take a quick look at each of the main types of gates. Later, we'll see how they can be used on actual devices.

NOT Gate

A NOT gate is a basic gate, not very different from the simple gate that we looked at in Figure 9.23, where there is an input, like a torch, and an output, such as the redstone itself.

Except in a NOT gate the circuit is always on, and flipping the switch turns the redstone off (**Figure 9.24**).

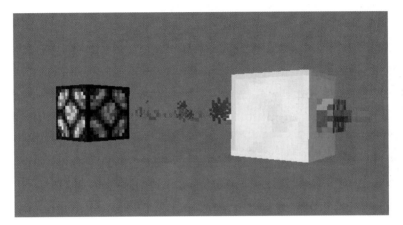

FIGURE 9.24 NOT gate.

Here, we used the redstone torch on the back of the block to change the signal When you use a NOT gate, you are making a circuit where the signal does NOT go through when the circuit is on. Using a NOT gate on your redstone device means that it is always on, until you use the switch to turn it off.

AND Gate

An AND gate (**Figure 9.25**) is pretty simple to understand—it needs two switches, and the signal will go through only if both are turned on. If only one switch is on, nothing will happen.

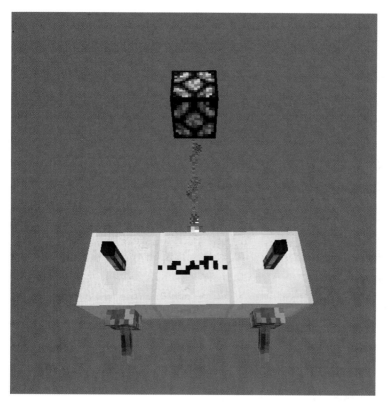

FIGURE 9.25 AND gate.

NAND Gate

A NAND gate (**Figure 9.26**) is like a combination of the two gates we just looked at. As with an AND gate, you need to use both switches to activate it. However, it is also like a NOT gate, in that the signal is always on, and so you must use those two switches to turn the device off, instead of on.

OR Gate

When there are two or more inputs and you can turn your device on with either switch A *or* switch B, we call it an OR gate (**Figure 9.27**). The only way to turn your device off is to make sure that *both* switches are off.

FIGURE 9.26 NAND gate.

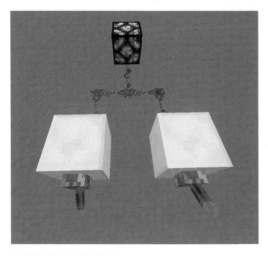

FIGURE 9.27 OR gate.

NOR Gate

A NOR gate (**Figure 9.28**) has two switches and will work only when both switches are turned off.

FIGURE 9.28 NOR gate.

XOR Gates

An XOR gate (**Figure 9.29**) is like an OR gate with a bit of a stricter rule. With an OR gate, the device will turn on if either of the switches is turned on—one or the other. An XOR gate will activate only if one is on and the other is not.

FIGURE 9.29 XOR gate.

XNOR Gate

An XNOR gate (**Figure 9.30**) works only when both switches are on or both switches are off. So long as both switches are set the same, power will be output.

FIGURE 9.30 XNOR gate.

Summary

This chapter is a very basic introduction to redstone before we move on to some awesome projects. You can find more information in electronics and computer books and online. The more you know about circuits both in and out of Minecraft, the more you'll be able to do with redstone.

16 Redstone Projects

There are as many redstone creations and devices as there are people to imagine them. From automated farms and brewing stations to complex defense systems, from various ways to lock your door to music systems and fireworks launchers, redstone projects can suit the tastes and needs of any player.

Wrednax (my 15-year-old) and I have put together these projects for you to try. Ranging from the very simple to the moderately complex, these projects will give you a taste of what you can make with redstone and allow you to gain the skills you'll need to experiment and create with redstone yourself.

Redstone Lamp

The most basic of redstone creations, the redstone lamp (**Figure 10.1**) is a simple light made from glowstone and redstone. Like glowstone, it gives off light that is one level higher than torches, but unlike glowstone, it can be turned on and off if attached to a switch.

FIGURE 10.1 Recipe for a redstone lamp, using redstone and glowstone.

Redstone lamps are easily powered to stay continuously lit by placing a redstone torch or redstone block adjacent to the lamp.

Redstone Lighting with a Lever

You can also power a redstone lamp with a lever, allowing you to turn the light on and off. Placing the lever in the block beside, above, or below the lamp will light up that one lamp. If you place the lever on the redstone lamp itself, all lamp blocks that are directly touching the lamp with the lever will also turn on (**Figure 10.2**).

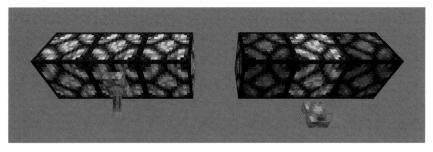

FIGURE 10.2 A lever placed directly on a redstone lamp (left) will also power the blocks touching it, but if you place the lever in a block adjacent to the lamp (right), it will power only that block.

Redstone Lighting with a Switch

You can add switches to your redstone lamps that are a little more complex than placing a lever directly on the lamp.

1. Place your redstone lamps.

   Here, we placed them in the ceiling (**Figure 10.3**).

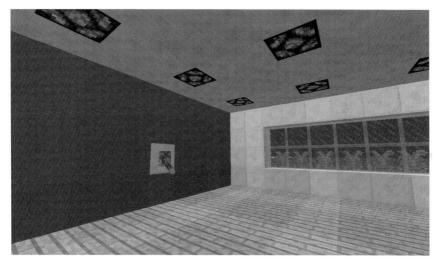

FIGURE 10.3 Redstone ceiling lamps activated with a wall switch.

2. Connect all your redstone lamps with redstone wiring (**Figure 10.4**).

   If they are more than 15 blocks from your switch location, you'll need to use repeaters to extend the current.

3. Place a wall switch (a lever), as in Figure 10.3.

   Since your switch is inside the room, and we want to keep the redstone wiring hidden away, we're going to run the redstone along the outside of the wall until it reaches the opposite side of the block that the lever is on (**Figure 10.5**).

4. Lay blocks in a stair formation (remember that redstone can't be placed on crafted steps).

5. Run your redstone down the outside of the wall.

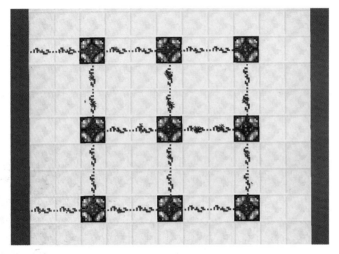

FIGURE 10.4 Connect all the lamps with redstone.

Here, we ran two lines of redstone wiring in order to reach all the lamps without needing a repeater. You'll likely want to have this area of your building blocked off when you're done, so that the redstone is hidden away.

Now that your lighting is wired up, you can turn your lights on with the flip of a switch.

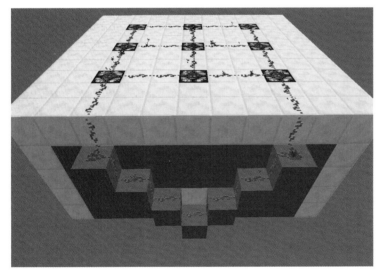

FIGURE 10.5 Use blocks in a stair foundation to lay redstone wiring that connects the lamps with the reverse side of the block that you have your switch on.

Redstone Lighting with Light Sensor

You can use a daylight sensor to turn your lights on automatically at night. This is a great option for lights set in the ground in walkways.

Daylight sensors are powered by the sun, and we want the lights to turn on at night. This is a perfect situation for a NOT gate to switch the current so that it is on at night and off during the day (**Figure 10.6**).

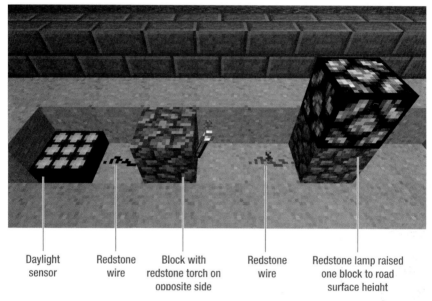

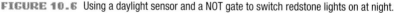

| Daylight sensor | Redstone wire | Block with redstone torch on opposite side | Redstone wire | Redstone lamp raised one block to road surface height |

FIGURE 10.6 Using a daylight sensor and a NOT gate to switch redstone lights on at night.

1. Dig down two blocks deep. This will allow you to cover the redstone wiring with blocks at your road height.

2. Place a light sensor two blocks deep into the ground.

3. Place a piece of redstone beside the sensor, leading to a solid block. Place a redstone torch on the other side of that block, creating a NOT gate.

4. Lay redstone from the torch to your lamp location (remembering that redstone signals go only 15 blocks). To raise your lamp to ground level, place a block under your redstone lamp. Fill in the road around the lamp, covering the wiring.

Doors

Doors are straightforward in Minecraft. You make the doorway and you place the door. Iron doors require a button, pressure plate, or lever to work, because they are powered, but you can simply place a button or lever. However, if you want to make more complicated doors, such as automated, hidden, or locking doors, you can use redstone.

Wiring a Door

Iron doors can't be opened without a power source. The easiest solutions are to use a button or lever beside the door, or a pressure plate at the base. Sometimes, though, you might want to hide a redstone wire in the floor, for times when you want to make a lock or open the door from another area.

You can open the door by powering the block underneath it (**Figure 10.7**). As long as the signal is less than 15 blocks away or you use a repeater to boost it, you can place the switch wherever you'd like, much like we did with the light switch.

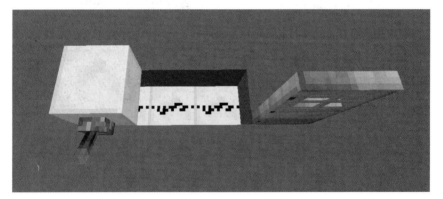

FIGURE 10.7 Run redstone wire underground to the block the door it's placed on.

Redstone Lamp Sticky Piston Door

This door uses sticky pistons to draw the door into the wall when a switch, such as a pressure plate, activates the redstone. While it can be crafted from most blocks, using redstone lamps as the doors (with redstone blocks forming the top and bottom of the doorframe) creates a flashy effect with minimal effort.

When the doors are closed, the redstone blocks power the lamps, making the door light up; as it slides open, the redstone lamps turn off because they are no longer in contact with the blocks.

This door could also be made in reverse by placing the redstone blocks above and below the blocks that the pistons retract into. And of course you can use almost any other blocks as well, to make a door that is camouflaged or decorative.

To make your door, you will need enough space for the doorway, the sticky pistons that will open the doors, and the wiring running underneath.

1. Working two blocks below where you will be placing your doors, lay the wiring for your door (**Figure 10.8**). You'll need to split the redstone wiring to reach the pressure plates you'll be placing on each side of the door.

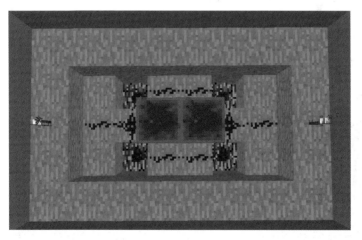

FIGURE 10.8 The wiring for your door. The two redstone blocks in the center are at floor height.

2. Add a redstone torch on each side to power the lower sticky pistons.

3. Place your door frame, doors, and sticky pistons. Sticky pistons can be placed facing different directions, so you will need to place them on their sides facing the door blocks. **Figure 10.9** shows the placement of the doors, the pistons, and the frame above and below the doors.

To power both the sticky pistons, we're going to need to power the block behind the lower piston.

4. Place a block above each redstone torch and a piece of redstone dust on top of those two blocks. This will power the upper pistons (**Figure 10.10**).

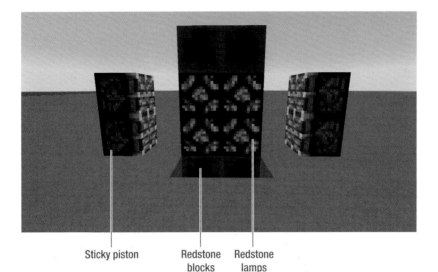

Sticky piston   Redstone Redstone
                 blocks   lamps

FIGURE 10.9 Redstone lamp doors, redstone blocks on the floor and ceiling, and sticky pistons. The pistons will extend and grab the redstone lamps when activated.

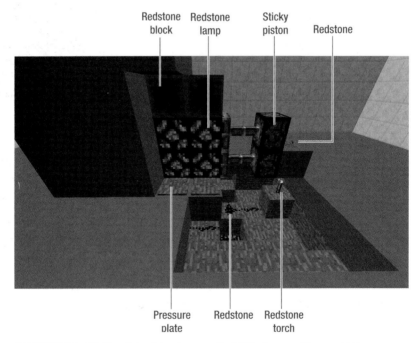

Redstone Redstone   Sticky
block   lamp   piston   Redstone

Pressure   Redstone Redstone
plate   torch

FIGURE 10.10 The sticky piston door—on the left the inner workings are hidden away, while on the right, we can see all the workings.

You can fill in the floor on either side of the door. Add pressure plates on both sides of the door and test it to make sure it works. Once you have confirmed that your redstone is functioning properly, you can hide the pistons and wiring in the walls and floor, as you can see on the left side of Figure 10.10.

Record Lock

There are various ways to lock your door. One cool method is to use a record lock, which uses a jukebox for the lock and a music disc for the key (**Figure 10.11**).

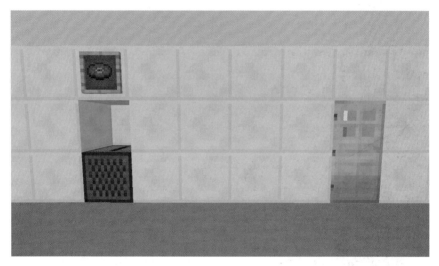

FIGURE 10.11 A record lock, here showing the music disc needed to open the door.

Every music disc generates a signal of a different length; for instance, cat sends a two-redstone signal, while ward sends one that is 10 blocks long. You can experiment to discover the signal of each disc, or you can find them on the wiki.

By using this information, we can connect a jukebox to a door, making the redstone wire the length of the signal associated with a particular music disc. To open the door, the player needs to have the correct music disc.

We'll be using repeaters to extend the correct signal to the door, and to block the signals that are too long or too short (**Figure 10.12**).

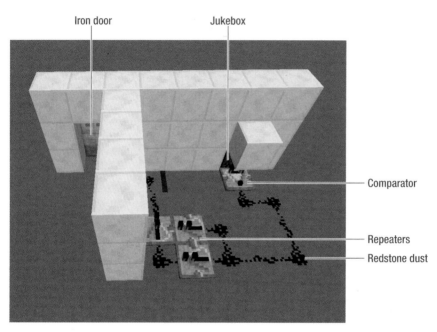

Iron door   Jukebox

Comparator

Repeaters
Redstone dust

FIGURE 10.12 Using repeaters to activate the door only when the correct disc is inserted in the jukebox.

In this example, we use the mall disc, which sends a signal for six blocks.

1. Decide where you are going to place your door and jukebox, and which disc you will be using. You will need enough space to lay a circuit the length of the disc signal between the comparator attached to the jukebox and the repeaters.

2. Place a comparator behind the jukebox. This will determine the strength of the signal, depending on which disc is placed in the jukebox.

3. Lay your redstone wire the correct number of blocks (here, it is six blocks, to match the signal from the mall disc) (**Figure 10.13**).

4. Place a repeater at the end of your redstone wire, and then place a second one directly beside it, connecting the two with a piece of redstone wire. Now place a third repeater connected to the second, facing toward the doorway (**Figure 10.14**).

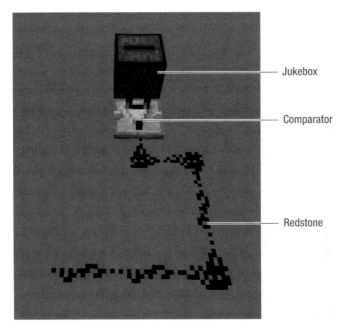

Jukebox

Comparator

Redstone

FIGURE 10.13 The jukebox, a comparator, and the six pieces of redstone wire needed to activate the door with the mall disc.

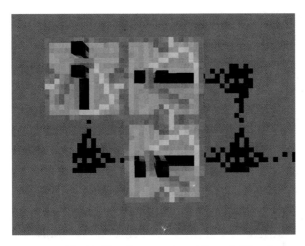

FIGURE 10.14 Place three repeaters at the end of the wire, to control the signals from the jukebox.

If the signal is the right length, it will end at the first repeater. If it is too short, it won't get there at all, and if it is too long, it will continue past the first repeater, to the second, where the signal will block the third.

5. Lay another piece of redstone on the other side of the first repeater, connecting it to the third. From there, lay redstone forward toward the door (see "Wiring a Door," earlier in this chapter).

Automated Pumpkin and Melon Farm

There are many ways to automate farms. We're going to look at a very simple system that uses redstone-wired pistons to harvest the pumpkins or melons, and water to direct them to hoppers (**Figure 10.15**).

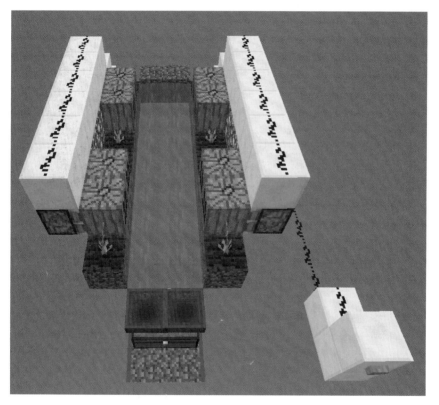

FIGURE 10.15 A basic pumpkin or melon farm is easy to craft.

Melons and pumpkins grow and are harvested in the same manner—for this tutorial we'll be using pumpkins.

1. Create your farm by placing two single-block-wide rows of dirt on either side of a water channel. Here, we're using packed ice (found in the Icy Plains Spike biome) to make the items move faster on its slippery surface.

   Pumpkins require two blocks of farm space for each plant—one for the stalk of the plant and an empty one for the pumpkin to grow on.

2. Hoe and plant your seeds in a pattern that will leave space for your pumpkins.

3. Place pistons behind and facing the spots you've left open.

   When the pumpkins are ripe, you'll push a button that extends the pistons, pushing them into the water (**Figure 10.16**).

FIGURE 10.16 The basic farm laid out without redstone.

4. Lay blocks above the pistons, running the length of the farm. At the far end of the farm, make steps of the blocks for your redstone.

5. Lay redstone wiring along the length of the farm and down the steps, adding repeaters to extend the current as it goes past 15 blocks. Make sure the repeaters are facing the right direction, so that the power is extended through them. Run the wire alongside your farm to the opposite end (**Figure 10.17**).

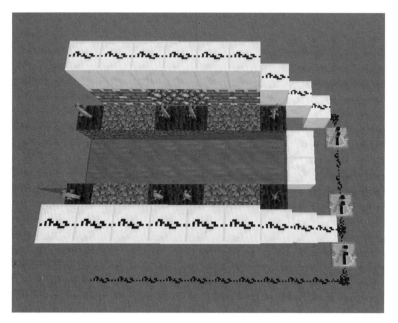

FIGURE 10.17 Place blocks over your pistons, and then run redstone over them to create powered blocks, continuing the redstone along the back and side of your farm.

6. Place a light source, or your plants won't grow.

   Here, we've placed glowstone blocks behind the plants, but you could use redstone lamps or torches as well.

7. Add a lever or a button to harvest your plants.

   Here, we placed blocks for a button, and ran the redstone to the back of the button block.

8. Add a double chest at the end of the farm, set into the ground, with hoppers connected.

   When you press the button, the pistons will extend, pushing the pumpkins into the water, where they are carried to the hoppers and deposited in the chests.

TNT Cannon

When it comes to redstone, what could be more fun than blowing things up? Cannons can be a delightfully destructive pastime, useful for self-defense or going up against others, or simply for the fun of explosions.

You can make incredibly complex cannons, but we're going to look at a basic single-shot cannon that launches on a time delay. Once you have the basics, you can experiment with other designs.

The TNT cannon has these components: a frame, water to ensure the cannon itself doesn't explode, and TNT for propulsion and ammunition.

> **NOTE:** When you're working with TNT, always make sure that you place it last, to avoid unpleasant accidents.

1. Build a basic frame, three blocks wide, with a half slab at the front. This is to help direct the TNT up at an angle, and to contain the water.

2. Add a block on the next layer, at the end. This will prime the TNT by powering it.

3. Place redstone along one side and one end of the cannon frame. This will activate the TNT when the launch button is pressed.

4. On the other side of the frame, place four repeaters between the TNT primer block and the redstone. Click the repeaters to shift the torches to be as far apart as possible. These will provide a signal delay before the TNT is launched.

5. Place a button on the back of the launcher. This will activate both the TNT and the launcher (**Figure 10.18**).

6. Place three blocks of TNT in the cannon, in the water. These will be the ammunition.

7. Place another piece at the front of the cannon, beside the primer block (**Figure 10.19**).

8. To fire your cannon, simply press the button.

To make cannons that fire farther, are more powerful, or even launch mobs or minecarts, experiment with cannons and look online for some of the many tutorials that go into more depth.

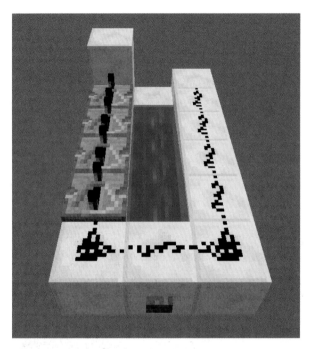

FIGURE 10.18 Prepping your TNT cannon—the repeaters delay the signal from the redstone, allowing you to get out of the way after you ignite the cannon.

FIGURE 10.19 Place your TNT and prepare to fire your cannon!

Fireworks Launcher

Fireworks are some of my favorite items in Minecraft. Hundreds of variations are available for you to make, and you can launch them easily by hand. A launcher filled with a variety of fireworks is extra delightful.

Simple Fireworks Launcher

You can make a simple or a very complex launcher. Let's start with a simple one.

1. Place dispensers in the ground, facing up, and place pressure plates in the front.

2. Fill them with an assortment of fireworks, and have your avatar run along the pressure plates to launch them (**Figure 10.20**).

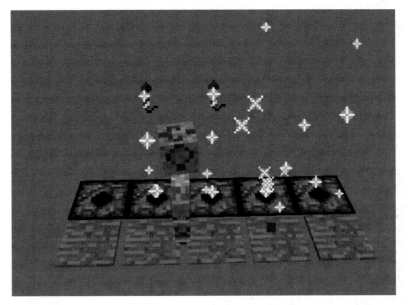

FIGURE 10.20 Wrednax runs along the pressure plates to launch fireworks.

The trouble with a launcher of this design is that although it is fun to play with, you won't be able to enjoy the fireworks as easily, because you must run back and forth launching them.

Repeating Fireworks Launcher

You can make a more complex launcher that sets off fireworks on a delayed cycle from a distance.

We are going to use a redstone clock to set the fireworks off in sequence. The clock is helpful for timing redstone creations.

1. To make a clock, you need to place repeaters in a circuit. Here, we've put them into a square formation.

2. Add dispensers at the corners that will launch the fireworks in sequence when the redstone signal reaches them (**Figure 10.21**).

3. Fill the dispensers with fireworks.

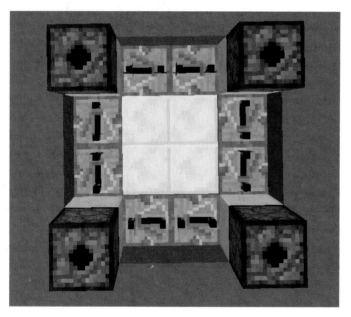

FIGURE 10.21 Redstone repeaters in a circuit that includes dispensers for fireworks.

To launch the fireworks, you can build a fuse that runs to the redstone clock and dispensers.

4. Lay a line of redstone from the repeaters to a launch button (**Figure 10.22**). You can make this as long as you need, just remember to add repeaters to extend the redstone signal for every 15 blocks of distance.

FIGURE 10.22 Make a launch button for your fireworks launcher.

Further Fun with Redstone

This has just been a taste of some of the amazing things you can do with redstone. Minecraft players have designed plans for many amazing redstone creations, such as completely automated farms, elaborate defense systems, cool games, and so much more. Players are constantly pushing the limits of what can be achieved with nothing more than redstone components and innovation.

Use what you've learned to practice, explore, build, and create with redstone. If you get stuck, check to make sure your circuit is complete, all your repeaters are facing the right direction, you have adequate power, and everything is where it should be. Take your time, pay attention to every step, and learn from your mistakes. The more you play with redstone, the easier it will become and you'll be able to do more with it.

Once you have the basics, expand your knowledge. Work with friends to share knowledge and to brainstorm. If you play on servers, ask more experienced players if they'd be willing to show you some of their work. There is also a lot of information online, and on the Minecraft wiki. Look for tutorials, let's plays, and directions for far more complex projects. As you explore, your knowledge base and skills will grow. Who knows—with practice, skill, and creativity, perhaps you'll become one of the experts that others come to for help and advice!

Glossary

API (application programming interface). A programming interface that allows software to interact or fit in with other software. In Minecraft, it allows for smoother matching of the programming with mods and plugins.

blocks. The basic building material in Minecraft, blocks are approximately one-meter cubes and can be anything from dirt and stone to wool or a watermelon.

caps. Using all uppercase letters when chatting online—it is considered shouting and therefore rude.

chunk. One section of the map, 16 blocks square and 256 blocks tall. Chunks are generated around the player as they move.

despawn. When a mob or item disappears from the game. Mobs despawn when they are killed. Player items dropped at death also despawn after a few minutes.

enchantments. Spells that can be applied to items by using an enchanting table and experience points.

End/the End. Another dimension in the game; populated by endermen and the ender dragon.

experience points. Points that are collected during gameplay by mining, smelting, killing mobs, and breeding animals; used for enchanting items.

forums. Online discussion boards on which people can post and reply to messages.

gaming servers. Hosted websites that allow gamers to join in a multiplayer game.

griefing. Deliberately damaging or destroying other players' work; may get a player banned from many servers.

grinder/mob grinder. A setup that allows mobs to spawn and be easily trapped and killed.

grinding. A system of getting experience points by killing mobs that spawn in a grinder.

hotbar. The accessible nine-item inventory that shows at the bottom of the main game screen and where each item matches a keypad number for instant access.

let's play (LP). A video of a gamer playing a game, usually with a commentary.

livestream. Playing a game live for an online audience, usually with a commentary.

mobs. Creatures in the game; mob is short for "mobile entity" and is a common gaming term.

mob drops. Items left, or dropped, by mobs when they are killed.

mob spawner. A dungeon cage that serves as a spawn point for mobs.

mods (modifications). Downloadable user-friendly additions or modifications to the game, usually written by other players.

Nether. The underworld of Minecraft—dark caverns filled with lava and hostile mobs.

NPCs (non-playable characters). Characters that are written into the game; players can often interact with them. Villagers in Minecraft are NPCs.

Overworld. The main world in Minecraft.

plugins. Software that changes or adds to the existing program on a server.

powered block. Any block that has been given redstone power (such as with redstone dust, a redstone torch, or a button or lever).

recipe. Directions for crafting items; often takes the form of a picture of the materials on a crafting bench.

redstone. A type of block that forms a powder used to make electric circuits; also the term used for the circuitry itself.

render distance. A game setting that determines how many chunks (sections of the map) are generated at a time. In the game settings, this falls under Fog, because the land becomes foggy at the edge of the rendered land.

reticle. The crosshairs in the middle of the screen.

resource. The API used by Mojang to install texture packs; now includes sound packs.

sandbox game. A game that takes place in an open world; the player has complete freedom to explore and create and isn't restricted to an existing storyline.

screenshot/screenie. Image taken of the current screen by pressing F2; saved in the .minecraft screenshots folder.

skin. The character's appearance in the game. The default skin is "Steve." Players can download or create custom skins.

smelting. Using a furnace to melt or reform an ore into another form, such as smelting iron ingots from iron ore blocks.

snapshot. Prereleased beta version of an update that players can download and try.

spamming. In game chat, swearing, repeating messages, insulting, posting links or web addresses, or otherwise annoying other players.

spawn. To appear in the game. Players and mobs both spawn; items can also be spawned into a game.

spawn point. The place at which a player first spawns; the spawn point can be reset by making and sleeping in a bed.

texture pack. A game modification that changes the appearance of all blocks.

vein. A cluster of ores, such as iron or redstone, that are connected.

walkthrough. A game tutorial, in text or video, in which a gamer plays through the game.

white-list. A system on servers where players must be approved, or placed on a "white list," in order to join.

wiki. A website that anyone can edit or add content to.

Index